Buildings for
Commerce and Industry

Buildings for

Commerce

Edited by Charles King Hoyt, AIA

and Industry

An Architectural Record Book McGraw-Hill Book Company

New York
St. Louis
San Francisco
Auckland
Bogotá
Düsseldorf
Johannesburg
London
Madrid
Mexico
Montreal
New Delhi
Panama
Paris
São Paulo
Singapore
Sydney
Tokyo
Toronto

Architectural Record Books
Apartments, Townhouses and Condominiums, 2/e
The Architectural Record Book of Vacation Houses, 2/e
Buildings for Commerce and Industry
Buildings for the Arts
Campus Planning and Design
Great Houses for View Sites, Beach Sites, Sites in the
    Woods, Meadow Sites, Small Sites, Sloping Sites, Steep
    Sites, Flat Sites
Hospitals and Healthcare Facilities, 2/e
Houses Architects Design for Themselves
Houses of the West
Interior Spaces Designed by Architects
Office Building Design, 2/e
Places for People: Hotels, Motels, Restaurants, Bars, Clubs,
    Community Recreation Facilities, Camps, Parks, Plazas,
    Playgrounds
Recycling Buildings: Renovations, Remodelings,
    Restorations, and Reuses
Techniques of Successful Practice, 2/e
A Treasury of Contemporary Houses

Architectural Record Series Books
Ayers: Specifications for Architecture, Engineering, and
    Construction
Feldman: Building Design for Maintainability
Heery: Time, Cost, and Architecture
Heimsath: Behavioral Architecture
Hopf: Designer's Guide to OSHA
Portman and Barnett: The Architect as Developer
Redstone: The New Downtowns

The editors for this book were Jeremy Robinson and Sue Cymes.
The designer was Patricia Barnes Mintz.
The production supervisors were Thomas G. Kowalczyk and Elizabeth Dineen.
It was set in Optima and Caledonia by The Clarinda Company
and printed and bound by Halliday Lithograph.

Library of Congress Cataloging in Publication Data

Main entry under title:

Buildings for commerce and industry.

  "An Architectural record book."
  Includes index.
  1. Mercantile buildings — United States.
  2. Office buildings — United States. I. Hoyt, Charles King.
  NA6212.B84   725   78-1421
  ISBN 0-07-002329-8
  1234567890 HDHD 7654321098

Contents

Contents (continued)

Contents (continued)

Chapter V: Industrial Buildings   152

Chapter VI: Industry-Related Buildings   190

Index   222

The Growing Importance Of Architecture And Design

As well as indicating new design directions for architects and designers, BUILDINGS FOR COMMERCE AND INDUSTRY is a direct response to the needs of business people, elicited by their many ongoing questions to the editors of the RECORD. The questions concern what kinds of buildings are being constructed to meet the needs of particular situations; who designs certain types of buildings; and what new feasibility considerations, such as energy conservation and human values, may now influence the decision to build in the first place. While the design professionals are familiar with the answers, business people often are not.

To answer the first two questions, this book shows a wide range of design solutions to problems typical in new commercial construction of every kind by leading designers. This even includes, in the last chapter, municipal facilities, such as sewage treatment plants, that must be "sold" to taxpayers and neighbors.

To answer the questions about new factors in construction feasibility, included are many concepts reflecting the vast changes that have come about in the last ten years or so—some of which are especially important to the business person.

Currently, important ideas about design are part of any new project's basic feasibility. First of all, new commercial construction is *not* automatically looked upon by communities as the "necessary evil" considered essential to a local dynamic economy only a few short years ago. It has become increasingly necessary for the developer of a store, office, or factory to convince a community's representatives that the developer's new building is really an asset to the environment, and that it "fits" with a newly awakened consciousness of where established communities should be headed as viable places to live and work.

The current community questions may be "is the new facility worth the cost in environmental terms?", and "does it produce local growth that is desirable?". Good design will certainly help alleviate concern over the first question, and hence may well influence the second.

Owners of new buildings themselves are learning to appreciate the benefits of good design without community pressure. Through their own new awareness of what good design can do for attracting business, through a new competitiveness in having a building of which to be proud, through the pressures of employees who want pleasant, safe places to work, and through newly enforced standards that represent local interests, many owners of new commercial buildings have come to realize the importance of how their buildings will function, and fit into their environment.

These three considerations—function, appearance, and "fit"—are, of course, those which have been of concern to most architects for years. And it is only through thoughtful design that these criteria for new commercial construction can be met. The benefits of function, appearance and fit will *not* be achieved by hanging decoration on a badly conceived box.

A real concern, when "design" is mentioned, will be cost. The fees for really good designers (especially if they are established) may and should be substantial. However, the quality of the design work will greatly influence the financial success of the project in a number of ways: by getting the new project accepted by communities without undue delays; by designing the new building so it houses activities in the most efficient, and therefore economical way; by getting it built as envisioned without costly design changes; and by providing the desired work environment, along with the desired visual messages about the business to prospective clients.

Clearly, having a good work environment and making an outstanding impression on clients have direct impact on a business's long-term receipts, and nowhere can this be seen better than in the first two chapters. While this is illustrated by effects on retail receipts, every factory owner is in a similar situation because the physical facility represents the product that is being sold.

The designer's fees, however, are a very small part of the costs in constructing any building. The most important question should be: "what does good design mean to construction costs?". The previously discussed, long-term economic benefits of a well-designed building might well warrant an initial expenditure above the bare minimum, but such an increase is not always necessary to produce a building of good design. This is illustrated by many new projects on the following pages. Great savings can also be achieved by the reuse of existing structures, a concept also discussed in this book. However, one area in which extra initial cost can show the most direct long-term financial gain is that of energy conservation, which should now be an integral part of any designer's considerations.

Of the great number of commercial and industrial buildings that have been built in this country without the help of talented design professionals, it has to be said that bad results can be just as visible as good ones. Extra moneys, if any, required to build buildings "right" are negligible when compared to the over-all cost of new facilities. The results will be with us—and especially with the owners—for a long time. And they will directly influence each owner'a pride, the attitudes of his or her workers, and above all *business.*

———*Charles K. Hoyt*

1
Shops and Boutiques

Clarity, boldness, intimacy, flexibility, complexity, economy, efficiency, and inventiveness. The qualities described by these eight words have a place in almost any design project—but especially in design for merchandising. Using outstanding examples that range from tiny boutiques in a New York department store to a revitalized 19th-century commercial block in Denver, this chapter attempts to explore the current problems and opportunities in store design. The first article, "Design for Merchandising," begins with the aesthetic aspects and continues through planning considerations to the practical problems which must be faced and solved if a store is to be a success. It is followed by in-depth coverage of specific projects that set new trends.

There are some matters in merchandising on which the designer has little influence. All too often the location for the store has already been chosen when the designer was called in, yet no other single decision does more to determine its future prosperity. The sales service offered is beyond his control. And the quality of merchandise, which can change so drastically over the life of a store, cannot be regulated by the designer, even though he may feel his taste ought to be the norm. It is just a coincidence, incidentally, that many of the shops included here sell goods with which designers would love to surround themselves.

What the designer can do is to restore to the shopper the sense of delight that a child feels when he runs into the toy department at Christmastime. After all, shopping should be fun for the customer. And shopping that is fun for the customer can be profitable for the owner, too. Many of the stores you will see on the following pages have produced much higher income than expected by either designer or client. Extra care pays off in design for merchandising.

DESIGN FOR MERCHANDISING: THE BASICS

No matter what else he does well, the architect who designs stores must be especially good at drawing customers in from the sidewalk. Agreed that location, service, and quality of merchandise are all important to a store's success, the attractiveness of the facade is still the most important design element. The four stores shown here have each solved the problem a different way but always with clarity: each design conveys the quality of the store quickly; each entrance is easy to find; each has a crystalline vitality that stops the window-shopper in his tracks—especially at night.

Le Dernier Cri, once a men's clothing boutique on the second floor of a Madison Avenue building in New York, took over the first floor space on the street in order to make its presence more obvious. Interior designer Allyn Berchin's solution, upper left, did that and much more. His simple, large-scale sloping exterior of stucco and glass prepared the approaching pedestrian for something special. But the real magnet was a sculptural staircase placed diagonally into the store and with a brilliant yellow panel extending all the way to the ceiling of the second floor.

Crate and Barrel, in Chicago's Old Town, right, had to be compatible with its somewhat over-preserved 19th century neighbors yet clearly say "contemporary design" to the pedestrian. Architect Richard Acott has used wood and warm masonry to make a good balance between the two. Although the entire facade is glass, the wood screen over the upper portion shields it from morning sun and yet is open enough for the two-story space to be apparent on the exterior at night. The clear light globes illuminate the sign but do not detract from the screen's transparency.

The crowded sidewalks of Madison Avenue near 57th Street in New York presented architect James Stewart Polshek with special problems as he designed the new Georg Jensen store. He has turned them to advantage by developing a design that concentrates the shopper's attention on a 14-ft-high band across the bottom. Below the bold logotype a multi-purpose show window (far right) is contrasted with a pair of silver-like metal doors covered by a large bas-relief of the Jensen crest. The scale of the displays in the windows is kept deliberately small so that those hurrying by see many objects freely placed, each speaking for itself.

Robert Mittelstadt's design for Streeter and Quarles West, a San Francisco sporting goods shop also placed in an old building, is based on maximum transparency. The brilliantly lit interior with its colorful merchandise is separated from the street by the least-obstructing glass wall possible. The enormous lettering on the window and on the transparent beam in front of it, the banner and the colors all draw attention to the store without diluting the openness of the design. Furthermore, the transparency of the new store, surrounded by a solid framework of classical architecture, provides a bold contrast with the other stores.

4.

1. Le Dernier Cri, Otto Baitz photo
2. Crate and Barrel, Bill Engdahl, Hedrich-Blessing photo
3. Georg Jensen, Van Brody photo
4. Streeter and Quarles West, Joshua Freiwald photo

1.

2.

CLARITY

GEORG JENSEN

3.

Boldness, long understood as an effective visual selling tool by roadside retailers, is the newest design technique in presenting high-quality merchandise. It does not always work. But when bold color and graphics are coupled with thoroughly disciplined functional and spatial concepts, the result can be a compelling magnet for those who respond to an exciting, up-to-the-minute environment.

Both of the shops on the opposite page use visual images in the interior which the shopper has first seen from the street. The giant photo-murals of sportsmen in action and vivid colors inside Streeter and Quarles West are used to draw people in. Then they guide them through a series of inter-related floor planes (see plan, p. 11) which might be confusing without such large-scale reference elements. The over-all effect, once inside the store, is quite restrained. But no matter, by then the brilliant colors of the sports equipment and clothing take over to attract the buyer's eye.

Allyn Berchin used the soaring yellow panel in Le Dernier Cri's staircase to not only draw people in off the street but to pull them up to the second floor where most of the merchandise was to be found. The powerful color and diagonal geometry of the stair contrasted with severely restrained colors and textures on the facade and the lower selling floor to heighten the customer's desire to go upstairs. The shop has now been modified for Halston.

Although Bonwit-Teller's Pierre Cardin boutique in New York, left, did have a door to the street, most customers entered it from the main floor of the store, unprepared for its barrage of color. One of an extraordinary series of specialty shops created by interior designer Harry Hinson for the Fifth Avenue store, this tiny boutique was a fitting jewelbox for the high-fashion men's clothing it contained. Mirrored doors were used on a continuous clothes storage wall along one side of the corridor. They effectively doubled the space, reflecting floor and walls covered with red goat-hair carpeting, purple ceiling and large bull's-eyes painted on ingenious hanging racks. The suits, in more subdued colors than those of the room, stood out against the ordered geometry of the design.

Woolf Bros. Subway, Kansas City is a living example of design reversing severe merchandising and functional problems. Located in the basement of an addition to Woolf Bros. on the Plaza, an extremely staid shopping center, the youth-oriented cavern has in fact become the busiest part of the store. Architect Norman De Haan's solution was to use very bold color and forms, left, along with a flexible fixture system to provide a space which can respond to the enormous changes that can take place in this type of retailing. The Subway also contains a fast-food restaurant, a dating center, a photography studio and meeting rooms to emphasize its interest in attracting and serving young people.

BOLDNESS

1. Streeter and Quarles West
   Jeremiah Bragstad photo
2. Bonwit-Teller, Otto Baitz photo
3. Woolf Bros. Subway
   David Phillips photo
4. Le Dernier Cri, Otto Baitz photo

1.

4.

There is not much a designer can do to produce intimacy inside a discount store or a supermarket; it's sad but it is a fact. Until recently, mass selling techniques seemed to be the only valid ones for future merchandising. But in the last few years, something has happened: whatever the reasons, and they range from moral to economic, people who once sought possessions in quantity now buy much more selectively. That means they shop more carefully, they pay attention to the quality of their purchases and they respond to the quality of the stores in which they shop.

Intimacy is a quality found not only in the tiny, off-beat boutique, but in any store which cares enough about the merchandise it offers to consider the feelings of the customers it hopes to attract. The selling spaces shown here are part of two New York department stores mentioned earlier. They are internationally known for their merchandise and their service. To continue that tradition and to broaden their appeal to newly discriminating buyers, each has developed a series of highly individualized selling spaces.

The B. H. Wragge boutique, devoted to women's sportswear, was another design for Bonwit-Teller's New York store by Harry Hinson. Around three sides of a 41-foot by 19-foot space adjacent to one of the large selling floors, upper photos, Hinson had built a series of closets, in effect, each two-feet-eight inches wide. During busy selling seasons, all of these niches were filled with clothes; at other times, a floor-to-ceiling panel, similar to those with paintings, upper left, and covered with the same fabric, could be placed over any niche, hiding it completely. The vertical white boards and the repeating panels formed a quiet but very functional backdrop for the sculpture and elegant furniture that the customer saw when she stepped off the elevator a hundred feet away. This inviting room, not unlike the living room of a spacious New York apartment, grossed an industry high per square foot from its start.

When Georg Jensen decided to leave their large Fifth Avenue store for less expensive space on Madison Avenue, they asked architect James Stewart Polshek to make every possible square foot of their new store productive without losing any of the elegance for which the store is known. His solution is full of intriguing ideas for any store designer. But the most pervasive is the sense of intimacy that comes from experiencing a continuous series of distinct spaces scaled to the merchandise. The lofty main floor with haughty floorwalkers is gone. Immediately upon entering a two-story entry, three floors are visible: the basement, far right, by way of a mirrored staircase; the main floor down a step or two and the mezzanine, left. The main floor and the mezzanine have brilliantly lit, very low ceilings above gleaming jewelry cases and furniture. Each of these spaces has its own character and seems, when one enters it, to be the only one in the store.

1. 2. Bonwit-Teller, Robert Riggs photos
3. 4. Georg Jensen, Van Brody photos

2.

INTIMACY

3.

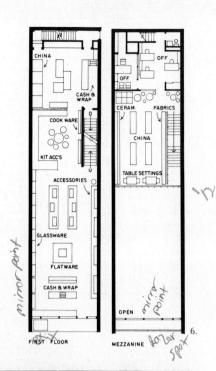

First handwritten annotations: "2/2 1 3/4 Larimer china square minor point by decimal spot mirro point cal spot"

1. 2. Larimer Square, Bruce McAllister photo
3. Georg Jensen
4. 5. 6. Crate and Barrel,
    Bill Engdahl, Hedrich-Blessing photos

CHINA
CASH & WRAP
COOK WARE
KIT ACC'S
ACCESSORIES
GLASSWARE
FLATWARE
CASH & WRAP

OFF
OFF
CERAM.   FABRICS
CHINA
TABLE SETTINGS
OPEN

FIRST FLOOR   MEZZANINE   6.

Flexibility in planning commercial space means not only easy changeability but also maximum opportunity for contact with merchandise by the potential buyer. In other words, in shops where the goods tend to sell themselves (and that is the case with all of the shops in this study), the more completely yet subtly the designer can move the consumer to all corners of the selling area, the more likely it is that the consumer will buy something on impulse. And even if he does not, a pleasant memory of moving about the store will bring him back again when he is ready to buy. Easy circulation, therefore is a most important criterion of good design for merchandising.

Richard Acott's straightforward plan for Crate and Barrel North, Chicago, a store specializing in elegant housewares and fabrics, allows the buyer to see each display of merchandise individually. The plan and view from the mezzanine, left, show how spacious the circulation paths actually are. Yet at the shopper's eye-level the room seems agreeably full without being cluttered. Thus, with extremely simple means Acott has accomplished a nice balance between the retailer's natural desire to display as much as possible on his selling floor and the buyer's natural desire to be free to browse—that is, to inspect the retailer's offerings without feeling undue pressure to either buy or get out.

The same principle of exposing customers to a maximum amount of merchandise, was used by Langdon Morris at Larimer Square, a block of 19th century buildings near downtown Denver. The original arrangement of stores, facing on the major street, top in the plan at right, with the rear as service area, has been substantially changed. Not only do some of the shops now open onto the alley, but in his renovation, architect Morris has developed a promenade through the middle of the block onto which many brand-new stores face. These very small boutiques specialize in unusual items such as candles, leather goods or stained glass objects. Of the twenty-eight businesses housed in the renovated block, twelve have new interiors and exteriors by the architect.

For the long, narrow upper floors of the new Georg Jensen store, James Polshek has done a system of display elements whose flexibility will provide a series of ever-changing small rooms in which to view china, glassware and the other accessories for which Jensen's is so famous. Dropped beams, which contain mechanical equipment and barely clear a tall person's head, span the narrow dimension of the typical floor. The multi-purpose U-shaped units shown opposite are designed to stack three wide between, and two high under the beams, thus permitting the display people at Jensen's to develop a high degree of enclosure between any two beams; in effect any floor can become a series of boutiques. Units can have adjustable glass shelves, sliding door hardware or integral lighting.

5.

4.

1.

2.

3.

FLEXIBILITY

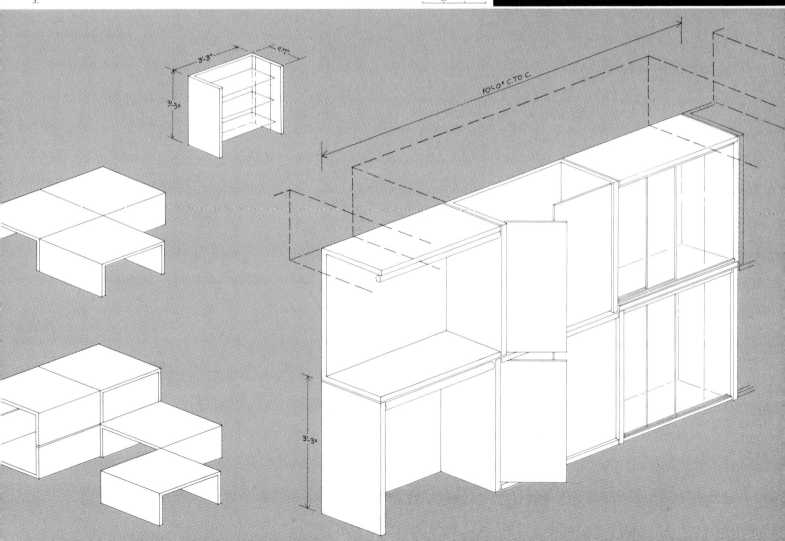

4.

It is not an accident that almost all of the projects presented in this Building Types Study are remodelings in one way or another. Recent economic trends have made many commercial clients re-examine their existing space and resolve to redevelop it for more intensive use. Furthermore, many marginal or abandoned structures are being thoroughly revitalized by careful renovations. The complexities which such projects present can seem insurmountable to the client's eye. But it is here, more clearly than in most construction, that the architect's ability to seize spatial opportunities, as well as to deal with structural anachronisms and functional problems, pays off.

In addition to its excellent planning, Larimer Square, Denver (opposite), is an example of complexity in renovation turned to advantage through emphasis. Instead of trying to hide the architectural idiosyncrasies behind a smooth new veneer (an unhappy common-place in the nationwide trend to reuse solid old buildings), architect Langdon Morris chose to reconstruct masonry walls and restore architectural details such as cornices, arches and columns. But where such refinements had never existed on the humble rear elevations of the buildings, he was free to build the new arches and openings that his mid-block walkway required in a less literal way. The lower-level courtyard with its outdoor cafe, opposite, required a certain amount of new masonry. The upper photograph illustrates the difficulties which the masons faced as they began their work; careful study of the photograph below it will reveal the sublety with which Morris integrated his new openings into the existing fabric. An interesting juxtaposition of old and new is a tie shop, bottom photograph on the mid-block promenade. It is one of several in Larimer Square completely designed by the architect.

A large but awkwardly-shaped volume (in what was once a major downtown San Francisco department store, now divided into several elegant shops and a parking garage), was the envelope with which Robert Mittelstadt had to work designing Streeter & Quarles West. The drawing, opposite, indicating a total of 24 feet between the lowest and highest levels, also shows how he developed "a series of 'floating' platforms that serve two functions: to provide a labyrinthine attraction for customers and to maximize the sales area." As the photograph on this page shows, the easy flow of the floor levels, one to another, could have a truly magnetic quality for the shopper. Beyond that, he has developed a series of flexible furnishings and fixtures to complement the spatial scheme. As the business grows, he finds himself still involved: tuning the lighting system, designing new fixtures and working with the sales staff on display set-up. But the basic conceptual framework of the shop, which grew out of careful study of the existing space by the architect, has proved to be the most flexible aspect of the design.

1.

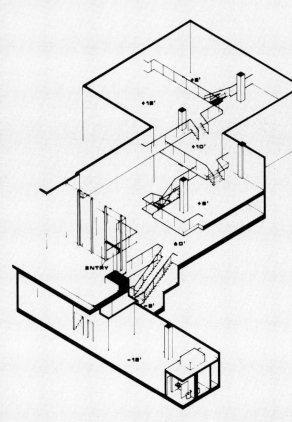

5.

COMPLEXITY

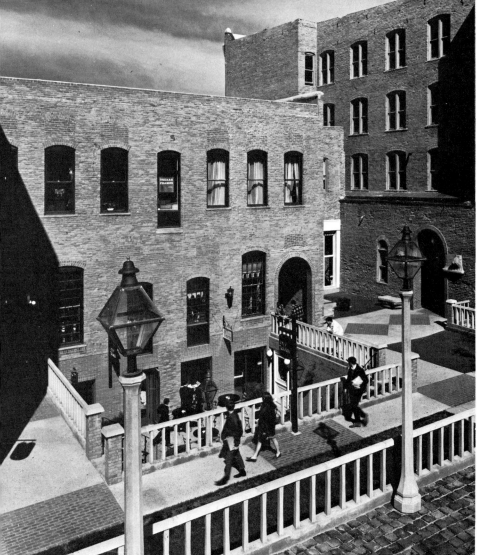

2.

3.

1. Larimer Square, Wayne Hecht photo
2. 3. Larimer Square, Bruce McAllister photos
4. 5. Streeter and Quarles West, Jeremiah Bragstad photo

ECONOMY

The big question is: how much should the merchandiser spend for capital investment or improvement? It is clear that for the store to be a commercial success, there must be a reasonable relationship between capital investment and future income. After all, economy really means spending wisely, not just minimally. One basic way to define the ratio of spending to expected income is to develop a "merchandising plan," in effect a financial program. By determining at the outset what parts of the operation will produce the best return, the allocation of space within the envelope of the total project can be made based on facts rather than whims or hunches. Past volume patterns, new trends and documents, such as the Departmental Merchandising and Operating Results of the National Retail Merchants Association (a collection of national store averages by departments), all can be used to determine the future volume of various parts of a new operation or to adjust proportions of an existing one about to be remodeled.

As cost estimates are being prepared for the amount of area or work the project will cover, both designer and client should remember that income will probably increase substantially as a result of the new work. In fact, the NRMA reports "volume increases of 25 to 35 per cent and more after modernizing an existing store, and from 50 to 75 per cent when enlarging and/or moving to a better location." There will be increased expenses also, of course, in rent, salaries, insurance, inventory and taxes. Another important consideration at this stage is the allocation of the total budget to the various parts of the job. The NRMA suggests that as much as 50 per cent may be allowed for the store front with 35 to 40 per cent for fixtures. They point out that each project has different requirements and offer these only as rough guidelines. But it is true that one of the architect's major contributions is to identify, early in the project, the total scope of the work required so that the owner can make provision, not only in terms of the budget but in terms of time, for the temporary operation of his business. All in all, completion of the project's economic design, before physical planning begins, will make the limits of the job very clear and will forestall later disappointments for both client and designer.

Several of the projects included in this study represent as careful economic design as space design. Le Dernier Cri is an example of an inexpensive and fast job which has transformed a business hidden away on the second floor into one of the traffic stoppers on Madison Avenue. With a budget that was low and a construction period of three months, the renovation, in its first year, substantially increased business over a similar period during the previous year. By focusing the money spent basically on the staircase and the facade, maximum effect was achieved with minimal means.

Robert Mittelstadt reports that although the design for the Streeter and Quarles West project exceeded the original budget (the construction cost was very low nevertheless) and the owner had to raise additional money, the response to the project and its merchandise has so far exceeded expectations that a profitable future is now assured. The question of whether a merchant should use an experienced store architect or, as SQW did, someone who has done no previous stores, is moot. While the experienced firm will no doubt come up with a more accurate financial program and thus building estimate, it is a real possibility that the fresh ideas of the beginner will compensate by producing a design with unexpected potential thanks to its reception by the public.

Harry Hinson, as director of design for the entire Bonwit-Teller chain, has had to deal with the problem of accomplishing new construction while maintaining business as usual nearby. He points out that alterations are more costly than new work and that alterations during continued business are even more costly. But loss of income during a total shut-down is even less desirable. So the simple, direct quality of his designs stems from the need to accomplish maximum change with simplest means as fast as possible. Thus to a degree that many architects would find uncomfortable, Hinson produces selling environments that are meant to change. Two levels of flexibility are apparent: the most obvious is operational adaptability as seen in the B. H. Wragge boutique, pp. 6 and 7. But in addition there is the idea that the whole area might be ripped out after a couple of years if merchandising trends change, and be replaced by another substantial but thoroughly different structure. While this approach might seem more akin to theatrical set design than to architecture, it proceeds in Hinson's case from the same thorough analysis of function and structural technique as any well-designed building and is all the more impressive for that reason. Ironically, it is a closer approach to the total flexibility that architects agree will be necessary in the future than many architects are now easily able to make in their own work.

2.

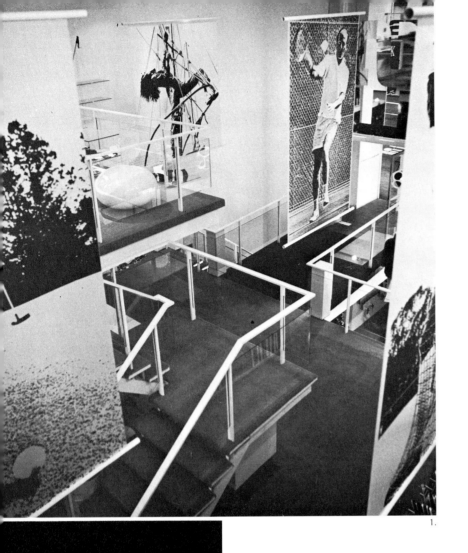

EFFICIENCY

1. Streeter and Quarles West, Joshua Freiwald photo
2. Le Dernier Cri, Otto Baitz photo
3. Woolf Bros. Subway, David Phillips photo

The store is a selling machine. Goods enter the building in quantity, must be inventoried and stored, then placed on the selling floor all with a minimum of effort. Programming for daily efficiency in operation is as much the designer's job as devising the seductive facade. And at best, the bold and clarified form of the store derives directly from a thorough analysis of how it will be used. There are three classes of users: the customers and the merchant-client, of course, but also the employees. They are, after all, the ones who will be spending the most time there. Adequate provisions for employees certainly will pay off in better service, an important consideration to today's shopper.

The National Retail Merchants Association, 100 West 31st Street, New York, New York 10001, is an organization that is interested in raising the quality of store design. In addition to a staff of experts available for consultation on various technical matters, the NRMA has recently published a book by architect Charles S. Telchin and Seymour Helfant, "Planning Your Store for Maximum Sales and Profit." For the architect designing his first store, the book is a concise primer of information relevant to efficient design. It is available through the NRMA.

One area often neglected by the designer, note the authors, is the cash and wrap station. Confusion and delay there can destroy all the pleasure of shopping in an otherwise attractive store. In his design for Woolf Bros. Subway, Norman DeHaan has made a very bold element of it, bottom photo. The circular form allows many customers to be serviced at once and provides a central information and control center, the focus of the store.

Another very important consideration in design of stores today, shoplifting prevention, is handled at Woolf Bros. in a flip but effective way. The closed-circuit television screens above the cash desk allow the young customers, says DeHaan, "to see themselves as thief or star." Thus the system becomes self-monitoring at the same time that it amuses those waiting to complete their purchases.

At Le Dernier Cri, unlike many stores, a policy of service only if the customer asks for it necessitated an unobtrusive means of control. The camera in the photo at far left covered the entrance and the stairway while another covered the second floor. Both were monitored at the secretary's desk. If necessary, power for the electric sliding door could be shut off by remote control.

An architecturally inconspicuous device, designed to detect goods from which a special electronically-sensitized tag has not been removed, has been installed at Streeter and Quarles West, top photo. The two white columns, three feet high and eight inches square and flanking the ramp near the entrance, ring an alarm and flash lights when an unauthorized attempt to remove merchandise is discovered.

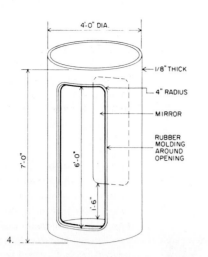

4.

1/8" THICK

4" RADIUS

MIRROR

RUBBER MOLDING AROUND OPENING

4'-0" DIA.

7'-0"

6'-0"

1'-6"

5.

INVENTIVENESS

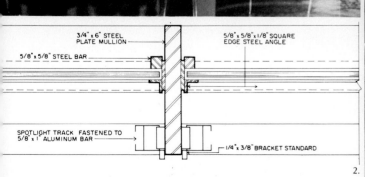

3/4" x 6" STEEL PLATE MULLION

5/8" x 5/8" x 1/8" SQUARE EDGE STEEL ANGLE

5/8" x 5/8" STEEL BAR

SPOTLIGHT TRACK FASTENED TO 5/8" x 1" ALUMINUM BAR

1/4" x 3/8" BRACKET STANDARD

2.

1.

6.

7.

Inventive detailing is the key to the truly effective, flexible merchandising environment. Simple and yet versatile details can be found in all eight projects in this study. In fact, almost any of the photographs will reveal the clever solution to a specific problem. But these next three pages focus on particularly intriguing examples of storage, display and especially lighting. The highly portable, bright red changing booth at Streeter and Quarles West, left, nothing more than a section of tubular fiber concrete form, exemplifies the best combination of bold ingenuity and utter flexibility.

Three quite different but equally straightforward examples of clothing display racks appear on this page. Each can be easily moved or modified as merchandising needs change. Each makes use of materials which, relatively simple in themselves, throw full attention upon the merchandise being displayed. Each puts the goods at the buyer's fingertips.

At Woolf Bros. Subway, top left, a system of chrome-plated industrial pipe structures, fastened to a ceiling grid, provides display fixtures that can be moved about easily and whose configuration of shelves, hanging rods and display panels can take many different forms.

Occasional tables of chromed-steel tubing became clothing racks when hung on the wall in Bonwit-Teller's Pierre Cardin Boutique. A brilliant bull's-eye design on white acrylic replaced the original glass top (see photo left).

Utterly open and accessible storage and display of merchandise is the basic design premise of Crate and Barrel, (see plan, p. 8). Architect Acott has provided, bottom photo, various types of fixtures on the mezzanine of the store, all hung from the wood ceiling. The tubes and hanging tables in the foreground, of acrylic sheeting, take little away from the merchandise itself and the warmth of the wood construction. As selling patterns change, these inexpensive elements can be easily moved or stored for future use.

A highly flexible lighting system is one of the most important aspects of design for merchandising. The new Georg Jensen store not only has such facilities throughout the interior but in its display windows as well (opposite page). To implement the small-scale window displays mentioned on p. 2, Polshek has designed a steel window frame that not only includes adjustable fit-

8.

1. 2. 3. Georg Jensen, Van Brody photos
4. 5. Streeter and Quarles West, Jeremiah Bragstad photo
6. Woolf Bros. Subway, David Phillips photo
7. Bonwit-Teller, Otto Baitz photo
8. Crate and Barrel, Bill Engdahl, Hedrich-Blessing photo

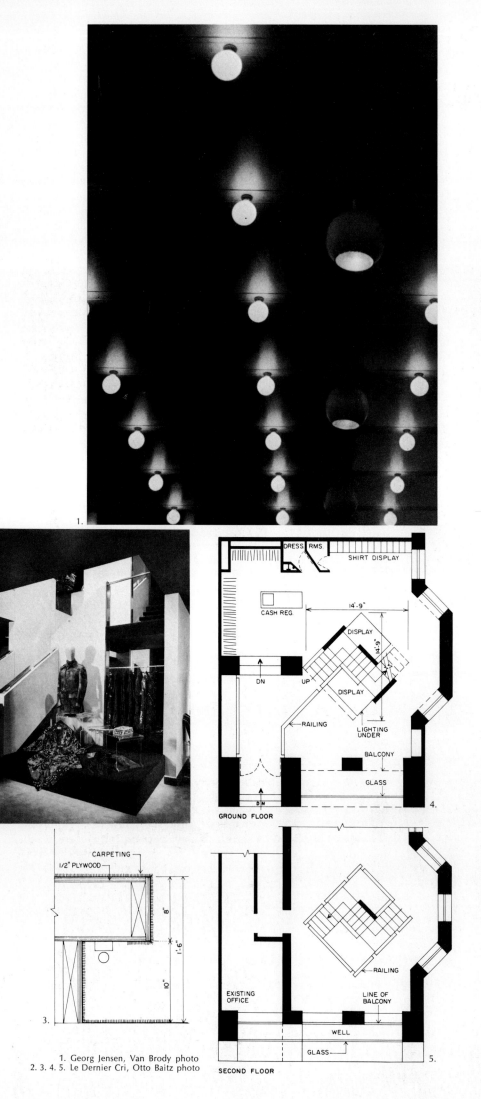

tings for shelves and display boxes but a concealed track and power supply for adjustable spotlights. Thus the window dresser has the means to put proper emphasis on the objects he chooses to display and the flexibility which will encourage frequent substitution of new objects.

In addition to the light beams occurring every ten feet on upper floors of Jensen's, the architect has chosen on the first floor and the mezzanine, very visible from the street, to emphasize the low ceiling, left, with a grid of small exposed bulbs, eighteen inches on center. In addition, at larger intervals, outlets for plug-in spotlights to highlight special pieces of jewelry have been provided. This system and the light beams are also shown on pp. 6 and 7. Actually, examples of flexible lighting can be found in almost every project included here, including a three-phase system at Woolf Bros. Subway: fluorescent two tube high output during midday; one tube low output in late afternoon and incandescent stage lighting only in the evening.

Lighting, this time with fixtures hidden, also played an important part in the design of the stairway at Le Dernier Cri. A simple detail, bottom left, made the entrance platform to the store seem truly to float above the existing floor, thus underscoring the effect of the new construction. An extension of the platform used for display, left, was the same size as the square cut in the floor above and also emphasized the juxtaposition of the new stairway with the geometry of the old store and Madison Avenue as well. The narrow stairway, emphasizing the intimate scale of the shop, worked well since relatively few customers were ever shopping there simultaneously.

B. H. WRAGGE AND PIERRE CARDIN BOUTIQUES, Bonwit-Teller, New York City. Owner: *Bonwit-Teller;* interior designer: *Harry Hinson.*
CRATE AND BARREL NORTH, Chicago. Owner: *Euromarket Designs Inc.;* architects: *Richard Acott and Associates;* mechanical equipment consultants: *Mechanical Design, Inc.;* general contractor: *J. A. Boulton and Co.*
GEORG JENSEN, New York City. Owner: *Georg Jensen Holding Co.;* architects: *James Stewart Polshek and Associates* — associate-in-charge: *Dimitri Linard;* project architect: *Joseph L. Fleischer;* project interior designer: *Nancy Jane Hertzfeld;* structural engineer: *Andrew Elliott;* mechanical engineer: *Jack Stone;* lighting consultants: *Kilpatrick and Gellert;* general contractor: *James Inman Construction Corp.*
LE DERNIER CRI, New York City. Owner: *Le Dernier Cri;* interior designers: *Allyn Berchin Design Office* — project designers: *Dave Snyder, Rena Kuhl;* mechanical engineer: *Ralph Caso;* general contractor: *Elan Construction Corp.*
LARIMER SQUARE, Denver. Owner: *Larimer Square Associates;* architects: *Langdon Morris,* associate partner, *RNL, Inc.;* structural engineer: *Vernon Winkel;* mechanical engineer: *John Blank;* electrical engineer: *Harold Dyer;* general contractor: *Kraft Building Contractors.*
STREETER & QUARLES WEST, San Francisco. Owner: *Michael Harrington, Inc.;* architects: *Robert Mittelstadt, Architect and Monte S. Bell;* project design: *Robert Mittelstadt;* structural engineers: *Forell-Chan;* electrical engineer: *Mel Camissa;* photo murals: *Lloyd Johnson.*
WOOLF BROS. SUBWAY, Kansas City, Mo. Owner: *Woolf Bros.;* interior designers: *Norman DeHaan Associates, Inc.*

DRESS. RMS.
SHIRT DISPLAY
CASH REG.
14'-9"
DISPLAY
14'-9"
DN   UP
DISPLAY
RAILING
LIGHTING UNDER
BALCONY
GLASS
DN
GROUND FLOOR   4.

CARPETING
1/2" PLYWOOD
8"
1'-6"
10"
3.

EXISTING OFFICE
RAILING
LINE OF BALCONY
WELL
GLASS
SECOND FLOOR   5.

1. Georg Jensen, Van Brody photo
2. 3. 4. 5. Le Dernier Cri, Otto Baitz photo

SHOPS THAT SET NEW TRENDS

In New York City's midtown district, a bookstore owned by the Museum of Modern Art demonstrates that a well designed renovation, in this case on one floor of a handsome early 20th century building, can be a profitable venture for the owner and still preserve the urban fabric of the area. The store has been so successful that it has recently expanded into space in an adjoining building. The architects, however, designed the store (while in the process of conducting a space planning study of all Museum facilities) under strict budgetary constraints, as the Museum's future expansion includes removing this building.

The architects integrated four separate spaces by adding doorways (replacing some bearing walls with partitions and steel lintels), thus opening up and interconnecting the spaces; and specifying the introduction of arched ceilings, an idea generated from arches seen on the exterior and throughout the interiors. The lighting system, designed to provide a high level of incandescent illumination at low cost, uses white porcelain industrial fixtures to light display areas, with smaller lights to highlight walls.

To make the store visible from the street, since the store's entrance is off the building's vestibule, an original wood door at street level was replaced with an all-glass one, permitting the passer-by to look into the vestibule and see a seven-foot-high partition announcing and guiding the visitor to the store. Two signs and a colorful banner were also placed on the exterior.

BOOKSTORE FOR MUSEUM OF MODERN ART, New York, New York. Architects: *Abraham Rothenberg Associates* and *Thomas Lowrie*. Engineers: *Robert Silman & Associates* (structural); *George Casper* (mechanical). Lighting consultants: *Howard Brandston Lighting Design Inc.* Contractor: *John Gallin & Son, Inc.*

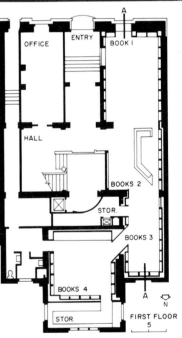

2

Located in a shopping mall facing an enclosed pedestrian street, this men's and women's hair cutting salon announces its presence by means of bold signage and a rear-screen projection system visible from the street. Customers are divided at the reception area by gender, then follow two separate but orderly routes through washing, cutting and drying (see plan). The women's areas, larger because of the preponderance of female customers, are broken down into several smaller volumes to make the spaces more intimate. The areas where the ceiling has been dropped are finished in metal pan. The high-ceilinged areas are covered in mylar and, in combination with mirrors and accent lighting, give these spaces a glowing, reflective character.

Working more or less within Vidal Sassoon's standards, the architects selected other finishes that are durable and easy to maintain: dark brown quarry-tile for floors, plywood cabinets covered in plastic laminate. Colors throughout are rather subdued in a conscious effort to let the materials rather than their coloration express the character of the space. Detailing is elegant.

The ambiance is dressy here and tinged with a glamor that seems not inappropriate in a place where style is a large part of what it's all about.

VIDAL SASSOON, Costa Mesa, California. Architects: *Gwathmey-Siegel*—*Tsun Kin Tam, job-captain.* Mechanical engineer: *Thomas Polise.* Contractor: *Illig Construction Company.*

Marvin Rand photos

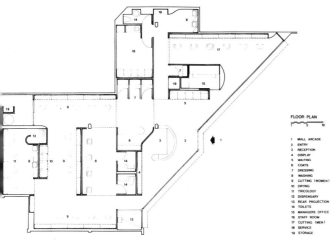

FLOOR PLAN

1 MALL ARCADE
2 ENTRY
3 RECEPTION
4 DISPLAY
5 WAITING
6 COATS
7 DRESSING
8 WASHING
9 CUTTING (WOMEN)
10 DRYING
11 TRICOLOGY
12 DISPENSARY
13 REAR PROJECTION
14 TOILETS
15 MANAGERS OFFICE
16 STAFF ROOM
17 CUTTING (MEN)
18 SERVICE
19 STORAGE

3

The MEC furniture showrooms in Tokyo specialize in modern international designs, and the building faces the Aoyama Dori, one of the
busiest streets in the city. The showrooms are arranged on three floors,
one at ground level (top right), one above, and one below (center right).
The interiors are elegantly inorganic and cool, finished in stainless
steel and marble and dark grey colors. Sculpted stairways (bottom
right) and openings from one floor to the next make a fluid and continuous space through all three levels (plans and sections below), and
movable metal partitions can open up or close off certain areas for
changing functions. These functions, in fact, are many, for the showrooms, with a bar and coffee lounge, are designed for sitting and relax-
ing as well as for buying and selling. Outside, the sloping chromium
mullions of the facade seem to be striving to express the kinetic qualities of the street, just as the glass reflects them. The architect, Paolo
Riani, attaches almost metaphysical significance to this reflectivity. He
points out that the front of the building is a "non-facade, made completely of mirror—a gigantic mirror. Here, therefore, the building does
not exist. What exists is only the reflected image—like the conscience—
of the reality that passes in front." What exists too is a stylishly complex
storefront that is, if nothing else, an eye-stopper to lure passers-by to
visit the elegant displays of the company's line of furniture within.

SHOWROOM OF MEC DESIGN INTERNATIONAL, Tokyo. Architect: *Paolo
Riani*. Interior designer: *Junko Enomoto*. General contractor: *Hazama-gumi Ltd.*

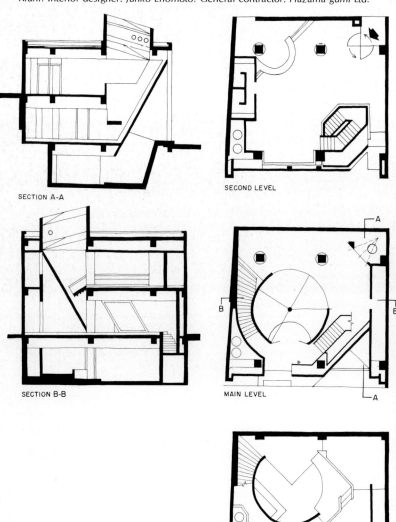

SECTION A-A

SECOND LEVEL

SECTION B-B

MAIN LEVEL

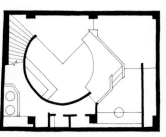

UNDERGROUND LEVEL

Kawasumi photos

Framed by a band of black concrete, a facade of mirror glass broken by slanting and horizontal mullions reflects the cars and people on a heavily trafficked street in Tokyo. The parallelogrammatic doorway is set back from the plane of the facade, which is broken again on the right to create a tetrahedronal void which drops down to the lower level of the building a complexity explained in the plans at far left).

4

When stores or shops or, in this case, wholesale showrooms are buried deep within a building—and therefore usually accessible only to people who know they are there—it becomes more important than ever to make them distinctive and therefore worth a visit. These showrooms are for Charlie's Girls and Hang Ten, two apparel manufacturers which are both divisions of a single larger company and are both serviced by the same office personnel. Here bold graphics have been introduced to attract the eyes of prospective buyers and to compete effectively with the other companies located in adjacent spaces on the same floor of the office building. In Charlie's Girls, an undulating wall—with the name of the company written both large and small on it—separates the waiting and office spaces (right and immediately below) from the actual selling areas (below right). For the greater part of its length the wall is formed by cabinetwork which houses the showroom's line of ladies' sports clothes, and these cabinets are lit from within by concealed lights. Along the window wall there are individual selling booths defined by freestanding panels with bars for hanging clothes (right). These panels can, when necessary, be moved aside for seasonal fashion shows to allow room for spectators and the processions of the models.

SHOWROOMS FOR CHARLIE'S GIRLS AND HANG TEN, New York City, Architects: *Robert A. M. Stern and John S. Hagmann.* Consultant: *Don Wise Advertising & Company* (graphics). Custom cabinetwork: *William Somerville & Company.* General contractor: *Chainin Construction Corporation.*

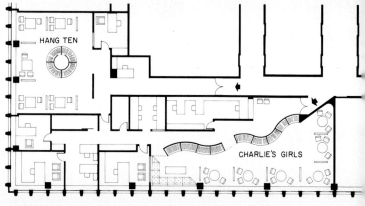

John Hill, photos

In designing the showroom for Hang Ten, a line of surfing and water-sports clothes, the problem of visibility was exacerbated by the long distance between the elevator hall and the showroom itself. The design solution (above) relies on the impact of a wall of abstract blue waves rushing towards two giant footprints—the company's logo—painted large on the far wall beyond the receiptionist's desk.

5

Antipathetic to yelling highway assertion, two Washington, D.C. stores by Hugh Newell Jacobsen fit quietly into their contexts of public benefit institutions by occupying found spaces. The blue all-carpeted surfaces of the Lincoln Memorial Bookshop occupy a previously seldom used 8-foot-wide V.I.P. "warming room" and now provide comfort for hundreds daily, while satisfying pressures of tourists for something to carry away. Originally quoting: "drive the money lenders from the temple," the architect wound up tackling the problem with gusto, even prescribing books vs. plastic souvenirs to be sold in the bright-on-dark sparkle and careful detail of jewelry hidden in its case. The museum shop of the Renwick Gallery maintains the character of its original exhibition room function, changed by sealing windows to provide security to the adjacent Blair House. Carefully lighted to avoid commercial glare, it asserts itself little beyond its strong green wall color and bright display cases. The latter are constructed of oak flooring and brass and would have well pleased the building's original 19th century designer in their materials and scale. Harmony is the watchword and it shows. In both stores the selling approach is probably most analogous to those more prestigious established firms who feel no need to tout their wares; the public will find them out no matter how discreetly presented.

LINCOLN MEMORIAL BOOKSHOP AND RENWICK GALLERY MUSEUM SHOP, Washington, D.C., Architect: *Hugh Newell Jacobsen.* Bookstore mechanical engineer: *Gaza Illis.* Museum shop lighting consultant: *Douglas Baker.*

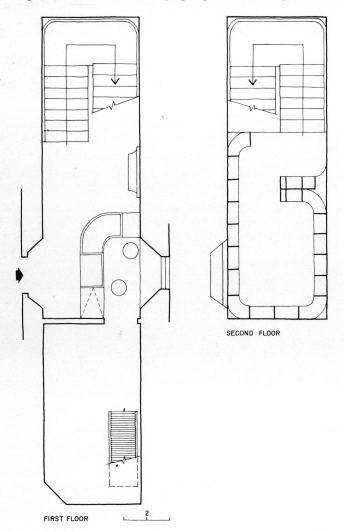

SECOND FLOOR

FIRST FLOOR

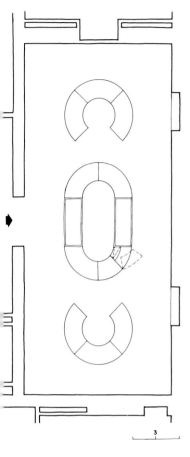

The Lincoln Memorial Bookshop (left) was created in an 8-foot-wide existing space and made double level (avoiding crowded clutter) by insertion of a new steel platform and stair. Dark blue carpeted surfaces and intimate lighting are an appropriate contrast to the light monumental space outside. The museum shop of the Renwick Gallery is treated as other exhibition spaces but specifically defined by strong green color (right). The brass and oak flooring cases would have well pleased the 19th century Renwick in their materials and scale. Flexible use can be seen by comparing the photograph and plan.

Robert C. Lautman photos

25

6

Orthogonality is a store which purveys a range of contemporary designs from toys and clothes to housewares and furnishings, and it is located in a remodeled commercial space 30- by 50- by 17-ft large. The architects reasoned that on an ordinary commercial street shoppers look more at the store itself than at the sign above it. Accordingly, Orthogonality's sign is understated, and what attracts the eyes of passers-by is the inside of the store and its merchandise, always brightly lit and highly visible. There is, in fact, no display window in the usual sense; instead the entire store is a display.

The only sign at ground level turns out to be the front door. It is a 5- by 9-ft piece of sculpted yellow fiberglass, with a big piece of rubber in it for a handle. This, according to the architects, is regarded by customers as very intriguing as well as a little freaky—so much so, indeed, that the yellow door has become Orthogonality's trademark and, in passing, has provided a less exotic nickname for the store. In warm weather, the yellow door stands open (above) and literally acts as a sign.

In addition to being a successfully straightforward piece of commercial design, Orthogonality is also an instance of a rather unusual mode of professional practice, since it was built by the architects themselves, with a crew of eight carpenters and the usual subcontractors.

ORTHOGONALITY, Birmingham, Michigan. Architects: *Brown/Steele/Bos. Inc.* Technical consultant for door: *McCoy-McCoy.*

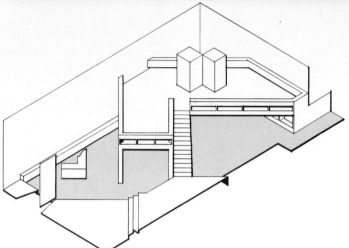

Greg Hursley photos

As a matter of taste, the architects were anxious to avoid using the faddish diagonal; they turned to it only when it become apparent that it was to their way of thinking the most effective way of inducing movement through the store. Customers are lured up onto the mezzanine by a series of gradually higher platforms that eventually bring the floor of the mezzanine to eye level (isometric drawing opposite page and photo above).

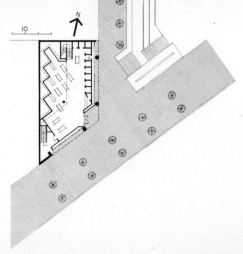

Philip Mòlten photos

7

Designed originally not for The Gap but as space for any kind of retail operation, The Gap found this space particularly suitable for its approach to merchandising casual wear clothes, and the store has proved to be one of the most successful in the chain. As one of the program requirements, the building was to be one story, meshing with the urban fabric of re-designed Market Street. The street, a main and heavily traveled thoroughfare in downtown San Francisco, is lined with commercial stores in a combination of old and new buildings, of varying heights—both high-rise and low-rise and is a major transit corridor for both buses and the only Bay Area Rapid Transit (BART) stations in the city.

The site is a corner lot facing a large, open area, with sunken plaza and entrance to a BART station, and a *cul-de-sac* for cable cars. To incorporate the building into the site, and not appear to be lost next to an eight-story building to the west, a sloping roof—the angle of which correlates to the grade at the BART entrance—visually continues the line of escalators and stairs. The store's entrance was placed at the corner of the building, capitalizing on pedestrian traffic along the street and from escalators and stairs. Circular columns add diversity at street level. Large display windows, slightly recessed behind the columns, have no mullions. Extra thick glass helps protect against vandalism in this much trafficked area of San Francisco.

THE GAP, San Francisco, California. Architects: *Bull Field Volkmann Stockwell—Daniel G. Volkmann, partner-in-charge; David L. Paoli, project architect.* Engineers: *GFDS Engineers* (structural); *Marion Cerbatos & Tomasi* (mechanical/electrical). Interior design and graphics: *The Gap.* Contractor: *Balliet Brothers Construction Corporation.*

A large, vertically framed skylight not only allows light to fill the interiors but adds a dimension of height to the building, maintaining the scale of the area, and adding a change in form at roof line. A blue roof injects color into the area, and since completion the neighboring building's open wall above the store has also been painted the same color, brightening the whole corner. For a small store, the interiors are quite diversified, with mezzanine level offering more and varied display space. The strong form of beams reflecting light from a skylight also adds a constantly changing pattern at ceiling height.

8

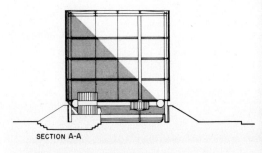

SECTION A-A

This small building of 1,000 square feet fits onto a corner site and offers a pleasant respite for the passer-by on a fully developed commercial strip area. Intended initially as a prototype (though the owner later abandoned this plan), the building's design was envisioned by the architects as a distinctive "floating cube" (30 feet square, 35 feet high) over a berm.

The building was built on grade and elevated on a concrete retaining wall which supports the berm. Four wood columns—each offset one-third the distance from one corner of each side—support a pinwheel roof framing system, which in turn supports a skylight roof (top and bottom). All four corners, therefore, cantilever off the columns. The roof skylight is stabilized with bracing, clearly visible in top and bottom photos. A continuous window seen just above the top of the berm gives the illusion the cube is floating while admitting some light above record display cases on the interior. The entrance is sunken, acting as a physical transition from the outside to an interior with a special image desired by the owners. Rest rooms and storage space are in a separate building.

The interior walls are mostly covered with redwood bark, with some sections covered with carpet to dampen reverberation of sound. The exterior is covered with cedar boards; copper strips were placed over columns.

THE RECORD STORE, Palo Alto, California. Architects: *Whisler-Patri—Piero Patri*, partner-in-charge of design; *Donald F. Atkinson*, partner-in-charge of production. Design consultant: *Thomas Aidala*. Engineers: *Hirsch and Gray* (structural); *Geo-Engineering Consultants* (foundation); *Yanow & Bauer* (mechanical/electrical). Consultants; *Gene Estribou* (acoustical); *Primo Angeli Graphics* (graphics); *Lee Saylor Inc.* (cost). Landscape architects: *Baronian and Danielson*. Contractor: *Ven Construction Co.*

Jeremiah O. Bragstad photos

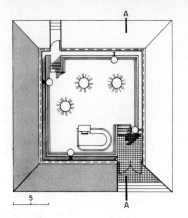

30

9

"The concept" of this store, according to the designers, "is an architectural inversion of the standard merchandising warehouse located in a suburban shopping center. The brick veneer of the facade and side walls was arbitrarily extended beyond the logical edge of the roofline, resulting in the disconcerting appearance of a building arrested somewhere between construction and demolition."

BEST PRODUCTS COMPANY, Houston, Texas, Architects: *SITE, Inc.—principal-in-charge and designer: James Wines; associate director of project: Emilio Sousa; graphics: Michael McDonough; associate architects: Maples-Jones Architects.* General contractor: *Conceptual Building Systems.*

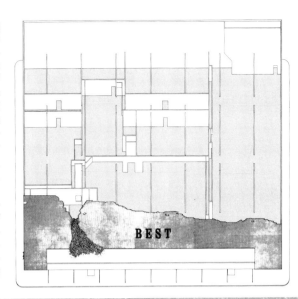

2
Shopping Centers and Department Stores

While the concepts of designing individual stores have been covered in the first chapter and will be expanded by individual examples on the following pages, the location of new department stores, and especially shopping centers, raises a broader set of issues. Generally, these issues revolve around finding or creating high volumes of shopper traffic.

In 1949 there were 49 shopping centers in the United States. Currently, there are nearer 15,000. Since department stores must be part of a busy shopping area to survive, they are often located in "shopping centers"—whether established urban centers or newly created environments. Where will new shopping centers be located? What will they be like? What markets will they serve?

It is increasingly likely that a sizable portion of new shopping centers will be located in the urban cores of this country, on sites that are small, expensive and in the center of dense development. Although regional shopping centers will continue to be important as retailing centers and as a building type, it is clear that a new glamour has begun to develop around "downtown" as a place to shop— and as a place to be.

The downtown location offers an all-but-forgotten market, one that has been there all along but which was overlooked in the rush to the suburbs during the 1950s and 1960s: the thousands who commute from the suburbs to work in the downtown areas, and the visitors and tourists who would consider a visit to a city incomplete if it did not include a visit to that city's "downtown." The market also includes the growing number of residents of the city itself, all of whom need, and presently lack, convenient, accessible, and attractive places to shop. It is a great untapped potential, and developers of retail facilities recognize it.

But these developers are a great deal more sophisticated than they or their predecessors were when the earlier centers were built, and they know that downtown realty is expensive, that it is scarce, and that to make a downtown project economically feasible it will have to create what one developer has called a "24-hour life style." This means shops plus other kinds of activities: restaurants, skating rinks, theaters, cinemas, hotels, office buildings, places for social and cultural events—places to meet the needs of a wide variety of interests and activities. Few, if any, shopping centers can, or would want to provide for all such activities, but any shopping center will benefit from proximity to existing or planned facilities that supplement their own.

An interesting phenomenon is that centers begun in an almost rural location often are quickly surrounded by urban development of considerable density. Not only does this happen in the United States—on the fringes of cities or within city limits—but Europe is experiencing this kind of growth as well. In an effort to control the type of development that takes place there, the French government has been acting as redeveloper for decaying suburban areas by selling land to private developers who build shopping centers as nuclei for future growth.

What began barely a quarter of a century ago in Los Angeles has, from all appearances, a strong potential—if well handled—to influence the future development of cities. On the other hand—as can be seen on the following pages—some retailers may find distinct advantages in established locations, and even in existing buildings.

New directions for downtown and suburban shopping centers

Some clairvoyants see the new downtown office-hotel-shopping mall complexes as catalysts for the revitalization of our cities, while predicting the demise of the suburban shopping center because of the changing attitudes toward using automobiles. In the first part of this chapter, there are four of the former and one of the latter, not because we agree completely with the prognostications, the implications of which are discussed in the accompanying text, but because these particular downtown centers are more interesting and instructive than the regional centers — with the exception of one which is included.

The conventional shopping center is a complete market place surrounded by or surrounding customer parking. It has a wide range of things to sell and a great variety of personal services as well as some very limited cultural and sports facilities. After parking the car, consumers walk to shops, department stores and dry cleaners. They can eat, go to the movies, play pinball or exercise themselves in the bowling alley. When they have had enough, they climb into their cars and drive home to their split-levels. The shopping center has served them in much the same way as Main Street serves their fellow Americans in older U.S. towns. The former boom in conventional shopping centers was directly related to the formerly high volume of tract housing construction. These modes of dwelling and consumption are intertwined by the motor car and now we are out of gas.

More and more shopping will be done by the worker en route to and from his job. Fewer and fewer trips will be made for the sole purpose of shopping, eating or recreation. The downtown shopping mall, accessible to public transportation if only by bus, will see wider use as the new complete market place. The noted shopping center architect Lathrop Douglass in an issue of the *Harvard Business Review* has called the largest and most complex of these "omnicenters" and predicts that we will be seeing a lot of them in the future. As a matter of fact we are beginning to see them now and the three completed shopping centers shown in this study—Broadway Plaza in Los Angeles, California (overleaf), Baystate West in Springfield, Massachusetts (pages 40–41) and the retail complex for Crown Center (which follows)—are all part of complexes which partially fit Douglass' definition.

Douglass believes that the sprawling, one-story centers in a sea of asphalt devoted exclusively to shopping services and limited recreation will disappear to be replaced by "multi-level structures with parking protected by the weather. Instead of today's typical one-level mall, the new design will have courts and malls at many levels to give the retailer maximum exposure. Other facilities will include motor hotels, offices, theaters, nightclubs, high-rise apartments, medical facilities and educational services."

According to Douglass, omnicenters will be built in the suburbs as well as in the central business districts and will appear most frequently in cities with populations of 100 thousand to 1 million. He cites as the principal reasons for their emergence, the scarcity and high cost of suitable land, and the need for shopping centers to be more competitive in terms of the range of facilities and merchandise offered. The United States now has more than 14,000 shopping centers and the average consumer (when gas was plentiful and thanks to our well-developed highway system) had a choice of several which were convenient to his home. Now he must be more selective as the centers become more competitive. Douglass believes that only the small neighborhood centers (similar to Meadow Mall in Simsbury, Connecticut) which are essentially supermarkets, will continue to survive.

He makes a strong economic and social case for the downtown omnicenter. He points out that these centers, if successful, as he believes they will be, provide employment and increase the tax base. The suburban omnicenter promises less obvious long-range benefits which are equally interesting. Because of stronger community resistance to shopping centers by citizens who now know what the word "ecology" means, and tougher Federal environmental regulations, the medium-sized center has become more and more difficult to build. The number of undertakings will diminish and land will be available for other uses. The suburban omnicenter has the advantage of using valuable land intensively. Its concentration of activities should encourage the development of public transportation in suburban and regional areas.

Douglass' predictions of financial success for the downtown shopping mall within an omnicenter are supported by current reports from Broadway Plaza designed by Charles Luckman Associates for the Ogden Development Corporation.

**The omnicenter can be
a financial success right from the start**
Except for the fact that architect Charles Luckman calls Broadway Plaza a megastructure rather than an omnicenter, as a new building type it fits the general category defined by Lathrop Douglass. Its astonishing success should help bring about Douglass' long-range forecasts. According to Charles Luckman Associates, the original predictions for the volume of pedestrian traffic and retail sales made three years ago for Broadway Plaza have turned out to be a gross underestimation. Before the center opened, Economic Research Associates estimated that an average of 18,000 persons would pour through Broadway Plaza daily. The actual initial average was 40,000 persons, and this was with the office building less than one-third occupied.

Over 4,500 cars enter the Broadway Plaza

1

Broadway Plaza in downtown Los Angeles is the nation's first urban center to integrate a hotel, office and retail concourse in one self-contained megastructure. The 4.5-acre, project, planned and designed by Charles Luckman Associates, is a joint venture of Ogden Development Corporation, Broadway-Hale Stores, Inc. and Urban Center Associates. Already a commercial success, it helps point the way toward the revitalization of the nation's central cities.

Broadway Plaza, in addition to its 250,000-square-foot department store (the first major department store to be built in downtown Los Angeles in 50 years), and its skylighted two-level galleria lined with specialty shops and restaurants, includes the 23-story, 500-room Hyatt Regency (the first new luxury hotel to be built in downtown Los Angeles in 20 years); "700" Flower, a 32-story, 773,000-square-foot office building; and a 2,000-car parking facility with six levels above the Broadway department store and two levels beneath the entire complex.

Designed to be a dramatic invitation to the inhabitants of "sprawl city" to stop driving all over the place and return downtown to enjoy the best of urban life, Broadway Plaza is experiencing unprecedented public response. There are high occupancy rates in the new hotel and the department store and shops are thriving.

As the site plan (left) indicates, the megastructure comprises an entire city block. Shown above is the principal entrance to the 50-foot-high two-level mall, which also appears in the photo of the hotel (opposite page bottom). The entire complex, including the office tower, can be seen in the bird's-eye photo (opposite page top). As the section (below) indicates the complex has four interconnected levels: "A" and "B"—the two lower levels— house the hotel meeting and banquet facilities, the employee facilities, subterranean parking, loading and storage areas and the central mechanical plant. The garden and plaza levels interconnect the mall, department store, office tower and hotel.

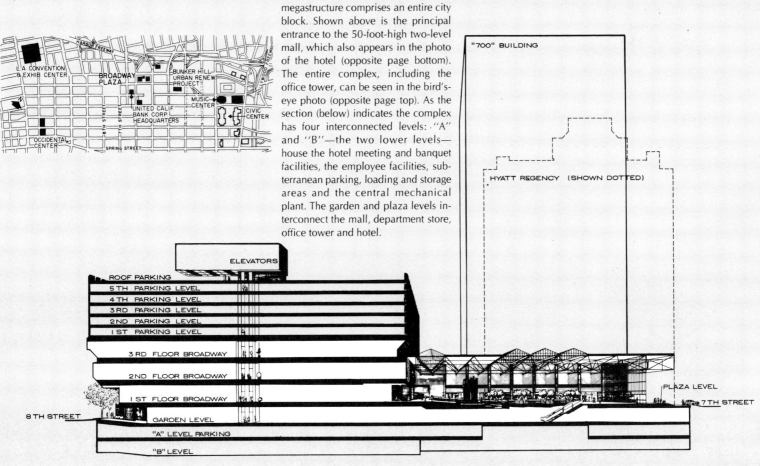

The skylight galleria roof is supported by visible trusses. Escalators and stairways lead from the plaza level of the galleria down to the garden level which opens onto the lobby of the Hyatt Regency (below left). According to architect Luckman: "Everything about the project was designed to provide an open, warm, inviting place for people. Extensive use of brick and wood throughout the two-level galleria, interior trees and flowering plants, benches, the fountain, the wide open store fronts, the flow of each element into the others—all were instigated by a desire to make this a hospitable place that says 'please come in and stay awhile.'" Daylight penetrates to the garden level and pool through the broad and spacious stairwell.

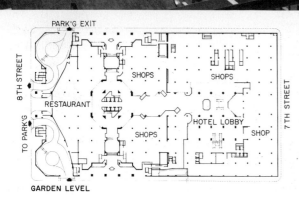

GARDEN LEVEL

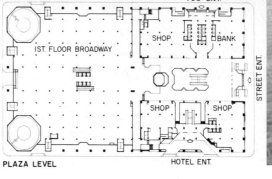

PLAZA LEVEL

parking structure daily and more than 50 per cent of this traffic comes from outlying suburban communities, including San Gabriel Valley, San Fernando Valley, Palos Verdes and West Los Angeles. The department store's sales in the first full year were 212 per cent over projections. Sunday traffic brings an average of 31,000 persons to Broadway Plaza and as a result the department store is open for business every Sunday as are most of the other shops in the retail concourse. The owners believe the gasoline shortage is boosting downtown trade, due to the availability of bus transportation to and within the central city. In addition, Broadway Plaza merchants are profiting from the new Sunday bus fares which permit passengers to go anywhere in Los Angeles for a single low fare. All of the retail tenants report business volumes far in excess of projections and complain that their most serious problem is keeping enough stock on their shelves.

Since opening, the Regency Hyatt Hotel has exceeded projections in all areas of operation — greater percentage of rooms occupied (56.9 per cent in the first eight months with many days of more than 90 per cent), higher room rates (average about $35.00), and food and beverage sales (total in the first four months of nearly $1 million). The total dollar volume for the hotel during the last of those months was $747,000, of which $457,000 was derived from food and beverage sales. Previous projections did not anticipate achieving $400,000 in food and beverage sales until the end of the following year.

Lunch business is booming. The lines are already too long from the customer's standpoint averaging 300 to 400 feet in length outside the more popular restaurants. Approximately 5,000 lunches are served on an average day throughout the complex.

Based upon its high volume of business, Hyatt has requested the owners to study and consider the addition of a third major restaurant and lounge area. The hotel banquet and catering services are also experiencing a far greater volume than had been anticipated. Preliminary "lost business" studies (banquet and meeting rooms all booked) indicate additional meeting and banquet space will be requested. Hyatt projected 80-85 per cent occupancy and had heavy convention bookings through its second full year, at the opening.

The owners and their architects believe that Broadway Plaza's success already is having a dramatic effect on downtown Los Angeles and will probably influence the future of other downtowns as well. The Plaza is making it evident to retailers that there is a downtown market in Los Angeles larger than most believed until now. It has been forcefully demonstrated that the increased rents which must be paid in a downtown complex are offset by greater sales volumes. Broadway Plaza proves that if a developer spends the money to create a public space downtown where people want to be, and if the architects and planner make the place attractive, people will come and spend their time and money.

Can a shopping center significantly improve the quality of urban life?

In the general spirit of eupohria which these centers arouse there is a tendency to overstate their importance in revitalizing cities as places to be. Although their economic and social value is obvious, in physical terms they tend to be self-sufficient and self-serving enclaves. This is the fault of the urban context in which they are built rather than a failure on the part of their architects, or a lack of vision on the part of their developers. The downtown shopping center within a megastructure or omni-center is potentially a strong shaping force and a major urban design element. Since none of the other downtown shopping malls shown in this study are located within an urban design framework comparable to Philadelphia's Market Street East, the latter will be discussed separately (pp. 118 and 119). Broadway Plaza can be reached only by private motor car, taxi or bus. As its site plan (p. 37) indicates, apart from sidewalks, there are no nearby pedestrian networks which link up with the shopping mall, nor does Broadway Plaza reinforce or extend an existing urban design structure of pedestrian ways and civic spaces. Few would seem to walk for the pleasure of it in downtown Los Angeles, and Broadway Plaza, shaped by circumstance into a self-contained entity, doesn't improve the world of the pedestrian until he gets inside. It is essentially an island of inward-turned amenities bearing no relationship except proximity by motor car to other developments in the area.

Like Broadway Plaza, Baystate West in Springfield, Massachusetts is also far less vital that it could be as a result of having been constructed without the benefits conferred by a well-conceived urban infrastructure imposed by the city to shape future development. Architects Catalano and Belluschi made the best of it, however, designing overhead bridges to connect the new mall with existing older department stores, and permitting the element containing the second level of shops to overhang the sidewalks, thus devising the semblance of a shaded pedestrian arcade. They created sunken gardens and other amenities, but the constraints were such that they could not bring daylight into the shopping mall. The latter consists entirely of artificially illuminated underground plazas and interconnecting shopping corridors.

The L-shaped shopping center at Crown Center (overleaf) serves as a multi-level pedestrian link, one leg of which spans a traffic artery to interconnect the office complex, the hotel and Hallmark Card, Inc. administration and production facility (another trendsetting project). Its architectural interest derives from the wit, style and playfulness with which such architects and designers as Francois Dallegret, Joseph Baker and Paul Laszlo have pro-

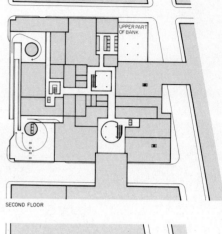

SECOND FLOOR

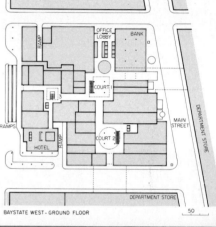

BAYSTATE WEST - GROUND FLOOR

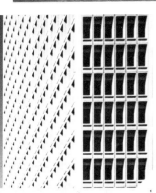

Baystate West was designed by Edward Catalano with Petro Belluschi as consultant in association with Crawley Cooper, Paul Shimamoto, Fred Taylor and Peter Sugar. It includes a two-level shopping mall and parking for 1,200 cars within an urban complex which includes a 270-room hotel, a 30-story office building, sunken gardens, paved areas, a swimming pool, fountain and a private club pavilion. The complex is joined by two enclosed bridges to two older department stores.

The shopping mall itself is formed by three artifically lit interior courts interconnected by short and narrow streets. The two larger plazas contain escalators which join up with the bridges to the older stores. The interior court (above) is square and uses mirrors as reflective surfaces. The 10-foot-square cube, proposed and designed by architect William Wainwright who served as a consultant to Catalano and Belluschi, is made of reflective acrylic plastic. It slowly rotates reflecting the dynamics of the spaces which surround it.

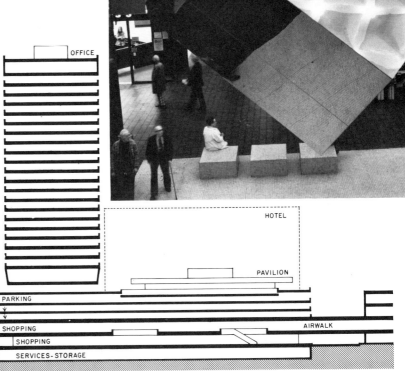

BAYSTATE WEST - SECTION

vided for the organization and display of a great variety of merchandise, and the freshness with which Harper & George have revived the idea of a farmers' market and designed a restaurant, rather than in the development of urban design concepts per se. Crown Center as a whole is a satellite rather than an integral part of downtown Kansas City and functions as a rival center in a Kansas City gray area rather than as a reinforcement of the downtown core. Its links with downtown are by automobile and bus only.

All three of the shopping malls just referred to and described in this study represent a high degree of commitment on the part of their developers to the idea that money can still be made in downtown retail. The spatial and functional complexity of all three required a high degree of programming and design skill on the part of their architects. Not one of them, however, had the advantage of being designed within a long-range urban design framework of the kind which the Philadelphia Planning Commission has been developing since the end of World War II and of which Market Street East is a key element.

Not one of them is part of a network of parks and squares linked by bicycle and pedestrian greenways to museums, landmarks and other places of historic interest. None is directly accessible by interurban train or subway. For these reasons, there are limits to the degree to which any one of them can truly revitalize the downtown areas of which they are a part. Shops, cinemas and restaurants opening off air-conditioned skylit malls which are linked up to parking garages fed by multi-lane expressways and crowned by towers agleam in the sun do not a city make—public relations claims to the contrary. People need a broader choice of leisure time activities than these highly sophisticated omnicenters offer. A person with a few hours off should be able to do more than shop and eat in a downtown mall. The shopping mall, although an essential element in a lively vibrant urban scene, must become part of a larger and more accommodating public environment. After 14 years of struggle by enlightened architects, planners and public officials, just such a mall is about to come to fruition—at Market Street East in the heart of Philadelphia, in conjunction with the project shown in this book under "Office Buildings," example 4.

3

A large specialty store which does not departmentalize its merchandise but groups it by "mood or lifestyle" (opposite page, bottom left) a shopping village (right) and a restaurant with seven cuisines (left) are the major elements in the new retail complex built by Hallmark Cards, Inc., for Crown Center.

The retail complex is an L-shaped, three-level structure with 400,000 square feet of space designed by Edward Larrabee Barnes who also serves as master planner of Crown Center. The interior of Halls, the large specialty store, was designed by Paul Laszlo Associates. The portion of the retail complex known as West Village (right) was designed by Francois Dallegret and Joseph Baker. It consists of cubical boutiques made of steel, plywood and glass arranged on two levels within a 32-foot high, two-story shell in which piping and ductwork is exposed. The farmers' market, called "The Market Place," covers 18,000 square feet and includes, in addition to the market stalls, a variety of special stores. Harper & George designed the restaurant and the market.

The Crown Center retail complex also includes 44 independent retail outlets. Among these is a general store (opposite page, bottom right).

4

Jack London Village is the latest retail shopping center on Oakland's waterfront and is part of the initial stage of an ambitious overall waterfront redevelopment plan by the Port of Oakland. The Jack London Waterfront Plan will eventually include office, hotel, residential and retail facilities and open space. The Village is built on 2.5 acres of a 5-acre parcel of land owned by the Port.

"The creative and technical world of the architect and environmental designer," says Frank Laulainen, the prime design force, "must stretch out to a world beyond the ordinary design solution to achieve a successful specialty shop environment, for both the visitor and the merchandiser." His design concept does achieve this special (and fun) environment that is not only an experience for the visitor who comes to get out of his car to shop, eat and walk around the waterfront (for this is the first time this land has been accessible to the public since the early whaling and shipping days), but profitable for the retailer, too.

The theme of the design was generated from the Port's criteria to build a new complex that is reminiscent of the rugged, robust days of an era in which Oakland-raised writer Jack London lived and wrote about it.

To accomplish this visually, yet provide up-to-date facilities for displaying merchandise, a small-scale, two-level complex, to be filled with specialty shops, restaurants, art galleries, craft studios and a theater, surrounds a central courtyard. All structure is wood-framed and wood-faced; heavy timbers are used throughout. The complex also has a fresh water pond, adding to the diversity of spaces and further relating the center to water. Spectacular views to the Oakland Estuary, Oakland skyline, San Francisco Bay and San Francisco skyline abound.

Opening a shopping center of

As a specialty shopping center, a variety of patterns—for visual effect and circulation—are experienced by the visitor walking around. Even though the complex covers a large area, it is not monumentally scaled, but adjusted to human scale. Retail shops and restaurant owners' desire for individual and different space are easily provided by the nature of the forms.

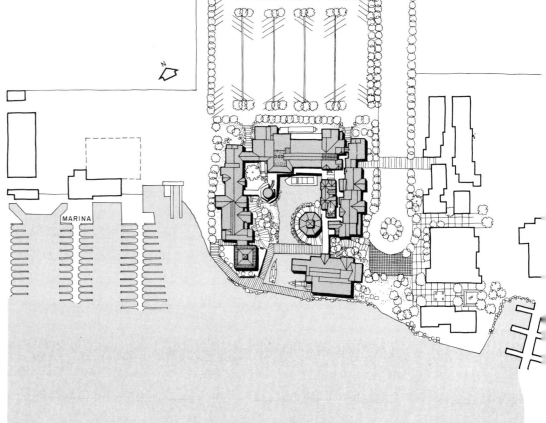

MARINA

this size in tenuous economic times indicates that the owner and developer felt the center could be an economically viable venture if designed as a "theme center." It has been able to successfully compete with other kinds and more established shopping areas.

The art of attracting shoppers is a combination of many factors—design, planning and use of materials. Outside the center, adequate parking is available. And future plans provide for shuttle service to and from the three main entries. Inside, the subtleties of design and circulation system guide the shopper through the Boardwalk (lower) level and lure him to the Vista (upper) level.

Variety is the key. There is not one straight, single flight of stairs, but rather split level staircases with landings, and both straight and curved ramps (also enabling the handicapped to move about). Walking surfaces are a combination of wood decking, cobblestone-textured concrete and pebbled concrete. One walkway wraps around the lagoon, connecting at one point to a public path (programmed in the waterfront master plan). Rest areas and open space were coordinated with view corridors, offering views to both water and other levels and activity.

The variety in forms (including gable roofs and turrets atop circular pavilions) also increases interest. A water tower, the tallest element, is the main identification and reference point.

JACK LONDON VILLAGE, Oakland, California. Architects: *Frank Laulainen & Associates.* Engineers: *Bradley Honholt* (structural); *P.R. McCoy* (mechanical); *Perry Cologne* (electrical). Landscape architects: *Larry Carducci* (initial phase); *Specialty Restaurants Corp.* Restaurant interior design: *Specialty Restaurants Corp.—Ron Wyle and Ted Cushman.* Developer: *Specialty Restaurants Corp.* Contractor: *The Geggatt Company.*

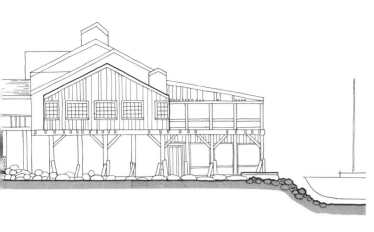

A total mix of forms, open spaces, materials, views, landscaping and interior spaces, combined in the right proportions and patterns have produced this new, exciting environment. Pathways and bridges vary in materials, as well as width. Some are wide and open (bottom, far left), some are under roof overhangs and some wind their way through smaller shops and display windows (top, right).

Spaces for larger stores, along with boutiques, are provided — many with angular ceilings, determined by type of roof and pitch. Clerestory windows increase use of natural light, and are yet another variation to visual form and interior space. Pavilions are used for restaurants and some shop space. Landscaping is augmented by marine artifacts, including a beached boat (center, opposite).

5

Architects Bull Field Volkmann Stockwell used a theatrical approach to modernize the outmoded Stanford Shopping Center in Palo Alto, California. Much of the work is like a stage-set design, creating not just a new facade but a new and festive atmosphere. Underlying such devices as new loggias, arches, outdoor display areas and graphics — all interconnected by an unusual framework system of bent pipe — is a new and ordered spatial development, enhanced by lush landscaping. It offers the retailer marketing flexibility while providing a vibrant and lively environment for the shopper where there was none before.

Gary Wincott

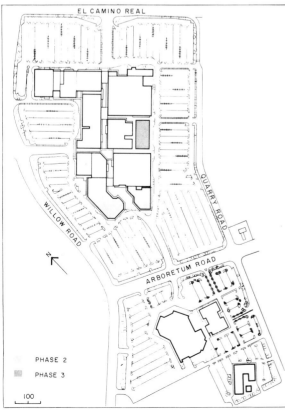

Jeremiah O. Bragstad photos except as noted

EL CAMINO REAL

QUARRY ROAD

WILLOW ROAD

ARBORETUM ROAD

N

PHASE 2

PHASE 3

100

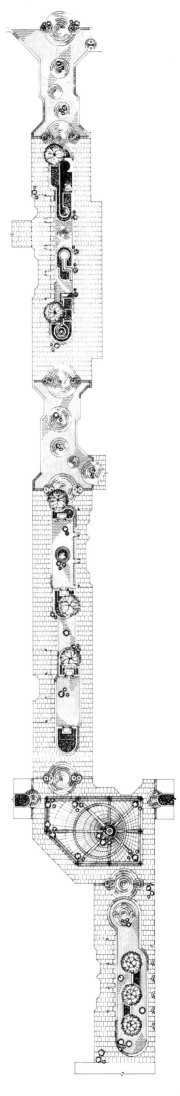

Stanford Shopping Center (owned by and located near Stanford University) was recently remodeled at an estimated cost of $10 million for three phases of remodeling and new construction. The design problem was clear: how to turn a 1950s-style shopping complex into an attractive, unified whole with renewed vitality; maintaining the existing structures and the linear mall, while creating new retail space. The architect's solution was to de-emphasize the multi-form structures, using them as a backdrop, and to center remodeling efforts on the 900-foot-long mall.

"The design concept was to create a sequence of spaces—a parade with a strong cadence and ceremony," explains John Field, architect-in-charge. It is this sequential experience highlighted by an incredible but integrated array of forms ¼in arches, loggias, fountains, awnings, landscaping and lighting—that has altered the entire atmosphere of the mall.

The main design device used to articulate the spaces and modulate the visual experiences is a dramatic change in scale from one area to another—producing a sequence of grandly and intimately scaled forms and spaces. The visitor rambles in and out of covered pathways along varying widths of the mall, around rusticated modern columns, landscaping, fountains and sitting areas, through the large volume of pavilion display space, and continually through arches formed from a bent-pipe framework system. The arches separate the different sections, and echo the Romanesque arches prevalent in the architecture of Stanford University. There is a further deliberate attempt to focus the shopper's attention on display windows by limiting the over-all background color scheme to muted colors; and yet by the positioning of arches directing views into other areas, the shopper is subtly enticed to continue moving to experience what's ahead.

REMODELING OF STANFORD SHOPPING CENTER, Palo Alto, California. Architects: *Bull Field Volkmann Stockwell—John Louis Field, architect-in-charge; Sherwood Stockwell, master plan architect; David L. Paoli, project architect; Daniel Chung, Gary Fong and Paul J. Meade, project directors.* Engineers: *L. F. Robinson & Associates* (structural), *Cooper Clark & Associates* (foundation), *Gayner Engineers* (mechanical/electrical), *Brian Kangas Foulk & Associates* (civil). Consultants: *John Smith* (shopping center advisor), *Frank Henry and Associates* (project manager for Stanford University), *Charles M. Salter* (acoustical), *William Lam Associates Inc.* (lighting), *Fire Protection Engineers* (fire protection), *Reis & Company and Intrinsics* (graphic design), *Clyde Winters* (graphic fabrication coordinator), *Peter Adamson* (cost). Landscape architects: *Fong & Larocca Associates.* General contractor: *Rudolph & Sletten.*

John Field

The shopping center, as designed in the 1950s (left and right), was laid out with a linear mall surrounded primarily by four large anchor stores. The redesign makes much more of the mall with semi-circular loggias, covered with bronze-colored acrylic plastic replacing corrugated aluminum walkway covers. Each loggia is lined with lights every 10 feet adding a sparkling quality at night. With the buildings painted muted tan and white colors, the only splash of color is in the banners hung from the loggias. These banners also break the long, linear view under the walkways.

John Field

John Field

The redesign of the Stanford Shopping Center encompasses all aspects of the complex but concentrates on the linear mall. Bull Field Volkmann Stockwell designed the standard, commonly used signs (e.g., sale and Christmas signs) and a graphics design guide. The main entrance (above) is emphasized by three 24-foot-high arches and an entrance court 26 feet high. Canvas awnings were added around the exterior to echo the inner mall characteristics. They also act as simple identification for the complex that did not previously exist. The mall design allows for maximum flexibility on the part of each retail store for design of its own storefront; whether it is unchanged from the initial center design, a prototype, or a new design, all fit under the loggia. In some instances, where there are large blank walls as a result of the initial plan, small specialty shops can be designed to fill the space without disturbing the circulation patterns. One clothing store (below left) was designed by the architects. The pavilion is a new space created specifically for outdoor displays. It is here that the only structural alteration occurs (original space shown in photo bottom right, opposite). The "grandness" of the columns results from the welding together into a cluster the pipes identical to those used throughout the center.

Gary Wincott

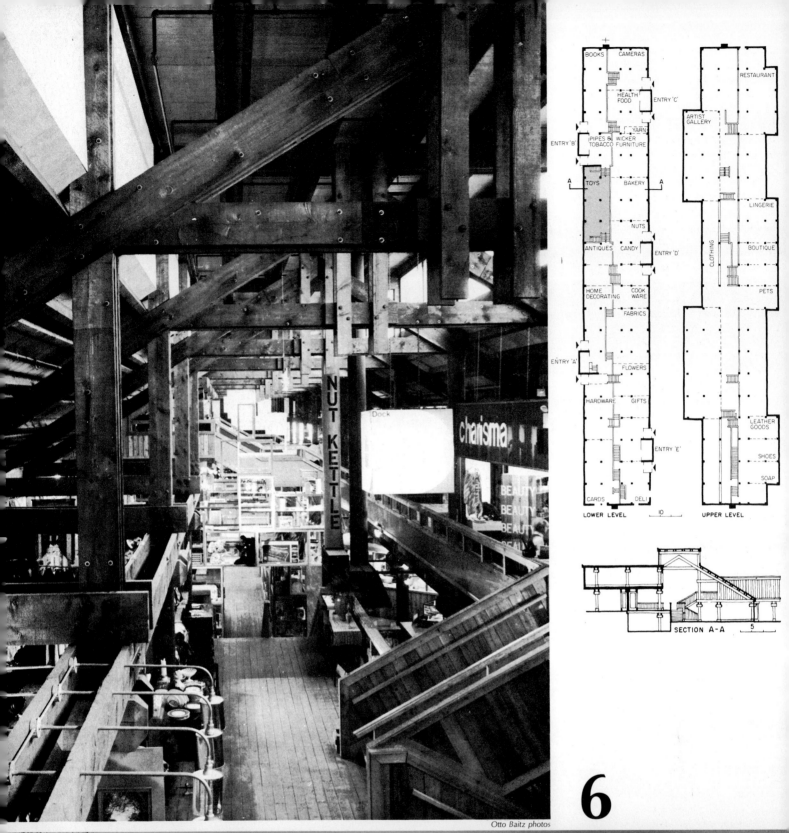

NUT KETTLE

Dock

chaisma

BEAUTY
BEAUTY
BEAUTY

BOOKS | CAMERAS

HEALTH
FOOD | ENTRY 'C'

YARN
PIPES &
TOBACCO | WICKER
FURNITURE

ENTRY 'B'

A | TOYS | BAKERY | A

NUTS

ANTIQUES | CANDY | ENTRY 'D'

HOME
DECORATING | COOK
WARE

FABRICS

ENTRY 'A' | FLOWERS

HARDWARE | GIFTS

ENTRY 'E'

CARDS | DELI

LOWER LEVEL | 10

RESTAURANT

ARTIST
GALLERY

LINGERIE

CLOTHING | BOUTIQUE

PETS

LEATHER
GOODS

SHOES

SOAP

UPPER LEVEL

SECTION A-A | 5

6

Otto Baitz photos

Since the innovative Heritage Village Bazaar opened, more than twenty small businesses selected by the Paparazzo Development Corporation staff have set up on the various levels of the building. Five boldly-lettered cubes hang in the space, and divide it into sections. Frequent maps key the various shops to the appropriate section. One of the most elusive charms of the building is the pleasant sense of confusion, of being overwhelmed with choice of things to see, samples to nibble, and crannies to explore.

Some of the shops, like the Nut Kettle with its orange roasting chimney, left, have modulated the entire space although most have fitted into the space with a minimum of additional construction. The most outstanding exception is the Carousel toy shop, right, by New Haven architect Caswell Cooke. Built of 150 brightly-painted 2x2 frame modules (18 by 36 by 54 inches) bolted together, the shop has an internal walkway which takes grandparents and others on a lengthy tour of the available gifts. At times the walkway rises twelve feet above the floor on which it is built. Conceived entirely in model form, the store was built within the Bazaar a module at a time. Except for a few specially reinforced sections such as the main stairway, the stacked modules support their own weight. A film was made of the one-day erection process including the reactions of several children turned loose on the newly built structure. Perhaps the best test of the flexibility of Callister's building is that another architect has been able to provide such an appropriate counterpoint within the framework.

The exterior of the Bazaar, designed in the now-familiar esthetic of the rest of Heritage Village, combines solidness and good scale with careful siting. The west side, right, forms one side of the Village Green while the east elevation, opposite, faces large parking lots.

THE BAZAAR AT THE VILLAGE GREEN, Heritage Village, Southbury, Connecticut. Owner: *Paparazzo Development Corporation.* Architects: *Callister and Payne;* associated architects: *August Rath;* structural engineer: *Glenn R. Nelson;* graphics consultant: *Barbara Stauffacher;* contractor: *Paparazzo Development Corp.*

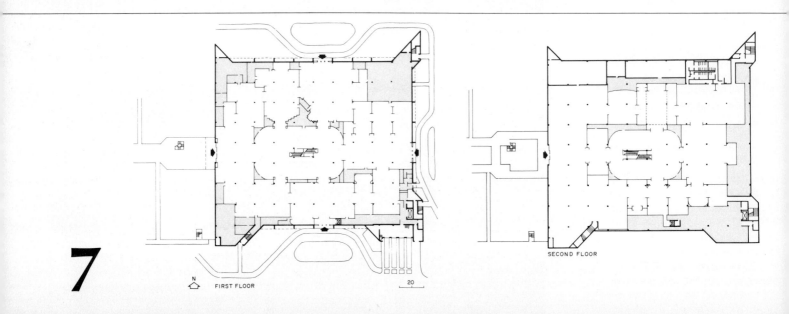

7

N
FIRST FLOOR   20

SECOND FLOOR

Aside from the large plinth-like structures at each of its corners, the facade of Burdines Department store is composed almost entirely of mirror-polished stainless steel panels that reflect the passing pedestrian and vehicular scene. The site for the department store is typical of suburban shopping centers, surrounded on three sides by vast expanses of parking lots. Landscaping is limited mainly to the periphery of the parking lots and to the area immediately around the store, so that there is very little to soften the visual impact of the undifferentiated asphalt surfaces. Accordingly, the unadorned facade with its large planar elements is appropriately at the scale of its immediate surroundings and makes a strong visual impact.

At nighttime, the facade of Burdines Department Store glows in the reflected light of passing cars; it is made of two-inch-thick, 30-inch-wide stainless steel and urethane foam panels. "Most of us think of building materials as static things, although there are certain things always happening with sun and shadows," say the architects; but this particular facade, in their view, "has a capacity for changing its mood and character—depending on the time of day and the kind of lighting, the sky, and the things that are happening all around it."

Inside, the store has two main levels of retail space (shown in the plans to the left) serviced by backstage supply areas (shaded on the plans) on each level.

The upper sales floor of Burdines Department Store in Tampa is reached by a centrally located escalator in a space topped with skylights (photograph below). Also skylit are the adjacent display cases, shown in the photograph below.

BURDINES OF FLORIDA DEPARTMENT STORE, Tampa, Florida. Architects: *Reynolds, Smith and Hills, Inc., Tampa office.* Engineers: *Reynolds, Smith and Hills, Inc.* (structural); *H. J. Ross Associates, Inc.* (mechanical/electrical). Consultants: *Walker/Grad, Inc.* (interiors/graphics). General contractor: *Frank J. Rooney.* Sub-contractors: *Fred McGilvray, Inc.* (mechanical/plumbing); *Flournoy Electric Co., Inc.* (electrical); H. H. Robertson Co. (stainless steel panels).

Henry O. Navratil photos

Marvin Rand ph

8

Bullock's is a chain of department stores in Southern California, most of whose newer buildings are located in shopping centers. This store in South Coast Plaza, a regional shopping center in Orange County, is in the city of Costa Mesa. It is the anchor store for the center and follows, in its exterior form, the precedent set by one of Bullock's earlier stores. Its walls are of ribbed weathering steel, with light-colored brick for trim and as a frame for entrances and a facing for some walls. Projecting elements break the length of the building and give it a distinctive form, something the client wanted as an identifying mark in the center.

The interior makes the most of the building's height by providing a three-story open space at the center. On each side of this great space are the escalators, with a dramatic view of the space and the several landings. The ceiling over this space is jet black and is studded with hundreds of clear-glass filament lamps set in crystal globes, and suspended at different distances from the ceiling.

General lighting in the store is minimal, provided by incandescent fixtures set in dark ceilings. Accent lighting from spotlights on a comprehensive system of tracks is used for specific merchandise and to focus on certain areas of the store.

Materials and colors for the interior were selected for their appropriateness to the casual living of the Orange County area: brick and roughsawn wood, earth colors, textured fabrics, and living—not plastic—plants. In the court, for instance, the escalator runs are faced with rough wood, as is the bow on the third floor which projects over the court; the two sides of the court are faced with heavy-textured brick set both flat and at angles. The floors at each landing are paved with octagonal and square tiles, and planters are effectively placed near the escalators. Carpet is used in the selling areas in colors appropriate to the merchandise: brick-red, gold, green blue, brown, red. Walls are treated in several ways—by painting, by use of graphics, and in the Fashion Gallery, silk damask as a wall covering. The architects designed all the interiors as well as all the graphics for the store.

BULLOCK'S SOUTH COAST PLAZA, Costa Mesa, California. Architects, interior designers and graphics: *Welton Becket and Associates*. Engineers: *Welton Becket and Associates* (structural); *Herman Blum Consulting Engineers* (mechanical/electrical); *LeRoy Crandall & Associates* (soils). Landscape architects: *Bridgers, Troller & Hazlett*. Contractor: *C.L. Peck*.

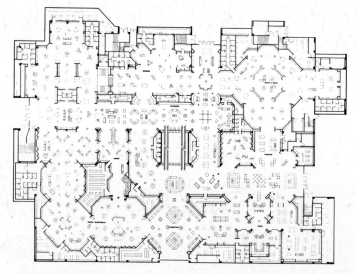

THIRD FLOOR PLAN

SECOND FLOOR PLAN

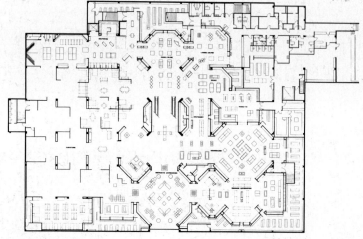

FIRST FLOOR PLAN

9

For the first time in its long history, Bergdorf Goodman—an elegant specialty store on New York's Fifth Avenue—has a store building designed to its own needs and desires. The new building is in the retail section of White Plains, New York, a fast-growing center (not a mall) for shopping which serves all of Westchester County, reported to be the "largest retail area in New York State."

Since this was the client's first experience with a project of this kind (the first store had been remodelled and added onto but was never a custom building for the client), the standards for the new store's program grew out of the reputation for elegance and service that had characterized the first store. Some of the physical amenities of the New York location also became requirements for the suburban site. In New York, for instance, Bergdorf Goodman is "on the Plaza" by the Plaza Hotel, and across 59th Street from Central Park. At White Plains, Bergdorf Goodman opens from a plaza which, like the Plaza in New York, has a distinctive fountain and is across the street from the park.

Inside the elegant travertine-faced building, everything focuses on a great open space covered by a 200-foot-long mirror-glass skylight which floods the store with light by day and at night presents a kaleidoscopic picture of colorful merchandise and movements of people below. This open space functions much as a street would—Fifth Avenue, for instance—providing circulation among and access to the boutiques which line its perimeter. The visual excitement produced by the great court overshadows the basic architectural function served by the covering skylight; to unify the diverse elements of the store, and in providing the means for understanding the whole store at a glance, to act as a constant orientation for the shopper. It is traditional elegance achieved without using traditional forms.

BERGDORF GOODMAN, White Plains, New York. Architects: *John Carl Warnecke, F.A.I.A., Architects*—project team: *A. Eugene Kohn*, partner-in-charge; *Emilio Arechaederra*, project director; *Laurence Goldberg*, project manager; *Stanley Abercrombie, Joe Owczarek*, designers. Interiors: *Eleanor LeMaire Associates, Inc.*—*Warren Hansen*, design director; *Vincent Caruso*, project design; *Naomi Leff, Jody Sayler, David Tredway*, designers; *Edward J. Agastino*, managing director. Engineers: *Ames & Selnik* (structural); *Joseph R. Loring & Associates, Inc.* (mechanical/electrical). Lighting consultant: *Douglas Baker*. Landscape architects: *M. Paul Friedberg Associates*. Contractors: *Conforti & Eisele*.

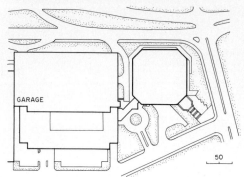

GARAGE

50

THIRD LEVEL

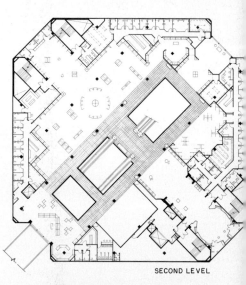

SECOND LEVEL

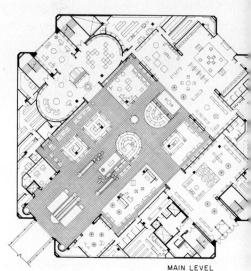

MAIN LEVEL

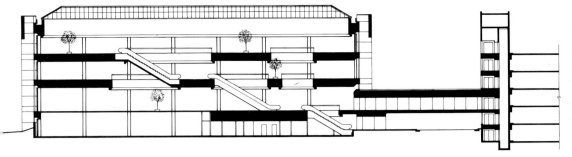

Escalators cascade through the open court on an angled line from topmost level to the lowest floor. Around the court or "street" are boutiques, shaped to the particular kind of merchandise offered and open to the "street." The boutiques are small, defined and intimate, but the over-all effect is an easy elegance, a degree of informality but never casualness. Fine materials play an important part in the quality of the store: marble and bronze are the principal materials used—marble for floors of general use (selling areas are carpeted) and to enclose escalator wells, bronze to cap and trim horizontal planes.

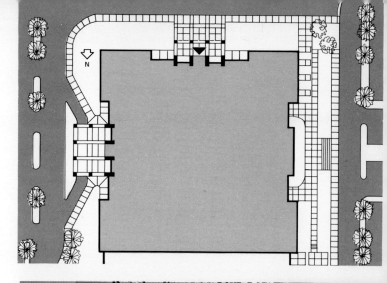

10

The store that wants to locate in an existing shopping center faces the problem of fitting its building into an established architectural concept with which it may not agree—for purely architectural reasons or because the design is alien to the store's identity—but with which it must conform. In such cases, the store and its architects rely on interiors of an exceptional concept to create an attraction strong enough to overcome what is, at least initially, the handicap of the non-identifying exterior.

At the Frontenac Fachion Center in St. Louis, a highly desirable retail location for a store of the calibre of Neiman-Marcus, the prevailing (and mandatory) design character was wholly out of character with the Neiman-Marcus image. The exterior of this new store conforms to the vocabulary of the center, but inside, with no impediments to design and expression, what the name Neiman-Marcus stands for is dramatically manifest. The elegant high fashion merchandise for which it is known is displayed with sophistication that enhances both the goods to be sold and the customer who comes either to buy or to look.

At the center of this essentially square building is a breathtakingly handsome "shaft of space," topped with a circular dome of mirror glass which daylights the area and much of the second floor. At night the mirror surface reflects the activity below, so that it is at all times a spectacular part of the store's effective environment. Since this shaft is also the space through which the escalator runs, it becomes a certain and unavoidable orientation for circulation between floors. Around the central "super space" are departments and boutiques with a variety of fixtures for display, with individual manners of setting off their merchandise from neighboring displays.

Although the central court or shaft appears to be an opulent use of space, it is cannily put to work as the location of the escalator circulation for the store, so that it is, in effect, considerably less a luxury than a handsomely executed necessity. Indeed, handsomeness is a key word throughout, expressed in the quality of the materials used, in the colors which differentiate departments and floors, and in a very special way, in the art works which owner Stanley Marcus has placed, as he has in his other stores, throughout this store. The works range in type from sculpture to needlework, from painting to macrame, and their subjects are equally varied. Displayed as part of the store's decor, and never as an exhibition, these

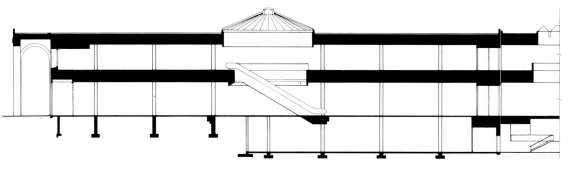

Besides the value of the mirror-glass dome as a focal point and an exceptional attraction for the store, the dome and the light it admits by day to the center of the building provide immediate orientation from any point on either floor. Not only is this two-story shaft of space both dramatic and luxurious, but the continually changing light, from morning to night, is itself an effective aspect of the store's decor. What it reflects from below at night again changes the effect of the interior. The store is large in area but only two stories high above ground, so one escalator only is used to connect the two principal floors.

Martin Helfer photos

Quiet elegance where elegance is called for characterizes the shops and departments in Neiman-Marcus' St. Louis store. At left is the men's department on the main floor; near right is the jewelry department, also on the main floor, where sculptor Ernest Trova's stainless steel "Gox" is on display. At far right is the girls' department, adaptable to the addition of color by display designers, while retaining its basic clarity of plan and detail. The Zodiac restaurant (below) on the second floor is basically a simple space made dramatically exciting by neon tubing and plexiglass as an attraction to its remote corner location.

works add greatly to the quality of the store's environment.

The materials used throughout are not only an embellishment of the store's interior, but are used with a subtle degree of functionalism: precast travertine terrazzo is used to state graphically the traffic pattern on each floor, whereas carpeting is used in each departmental sales area. The travertine terrazzo, made in two shades of beige, in Italy, in pieces large enough to emphasize the scale of the spaces in the store, provides an instantly recognizable identification for each boutique or shop, and the carpeting, in special colors developed for this store, invites the customer into the sales area. In certain departments—the second floor fashion department, for instance—custom designs are made for both carpeting and for the printed fabrics used on the walls. Elsewhere, stock designs in special colors, clear and fresh, are used. Acrylic sheet materials are used on the walls of the children's department. Where wood is used, it is left natural.

The design team that worked out the concept for this store represents the coordination of two design offices: the architectural firm and the interior design firm which is its subsidiary, an unusual conjunction but one which worked well together to produce a harmonious integration of space, color and materials. Long-continued studies of the merchandising field have led to participation by the interior designers in the decisions made by the store management on the location and juxtaposition of departments as well as on the design of the interiors. Since Neiman-Marcus stores have a policy of not identifying by signs either departments or merchandise, the interrelation of design and merchandise display is of particular importance in the successful operation of the store.

NEIMAN-MARCUS, Frontenac Fashion Center, St. Louis, Missouri Architect: *John Carl Warnecke, F.A.I.A., Architects—A. Eugene Kohn,* partner-in-charge; *Emilio Arechaederra,* director of store division; *Guillermo Loos,* project director; *Laurence Goldberg,* project manager; *Stanley Abercrombie, Joe Owczarek,* designers. Interiors: *Eleanor LeMaire Associates, Inc.—Robert A. Malderez,* design director; *Frank J. LaBianca,* project designer; *Henry J. Wilson, Jim Robertson, Cindy Collins,* staff designers; *Edward J. Agostino,* managing director. Engineers: *Harald Nielsen & Associates, Inc.* (structural); *Magill-Cloud Engineers, Inc.* (mechanical/electrical). Lighting consultant: *Douglas Baker.* Contractor: *Gamble Construction Company.*

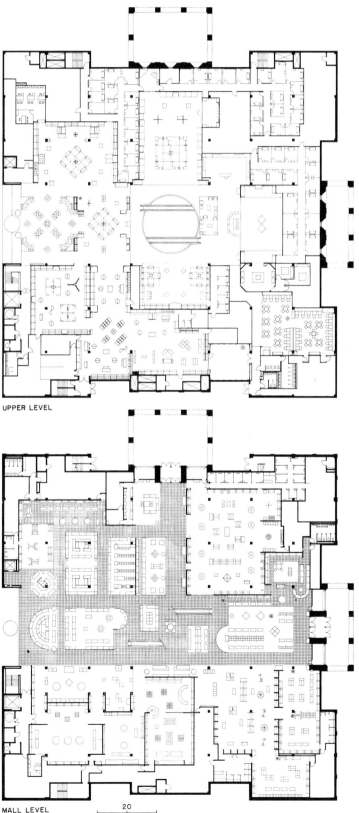

UPPER LEVEL

MALL LEVEL   20

11

Built on a four-acre site near an expressway, this lumber company is designed to serve do-it-yourself customers as well as contractors. For the individual customers there is a large parking lot in front of the building, and at the side are separate entrances for contractors and employees. The area roofed in by a series of dramatic wood trusses is nearly an acre, and of this about 12,000 square feet are devoted to retail sales. Bays of 54 by 32 feet were used to provide maximum flexibility and for future expansion. The ceiling height of 17 feet to the underside of the trusses is dictated by the stacking requirements of the warehouse area and by certain two-story areas in the retail sales part of the building. All of the trusses, columns, wall and roof panels were prefabricated from structural lumber, finished naturally, with exposed metal connectors. The architects' idea was to design a straightforward commercial facility that they hoped might recall the ordinary warehouse buildings that lumber companies usually are. In doing this, though, they have also made a structure whose presence turns out to be extraordinary and acts as a powerful magnet to attract shoppers. It is also a highly sophisticated variant from the usual highway magnets for motorists.

NAGLE LUMBER COMPANY, Iowa City, Iowa. Architects: *Booth and Nagle—associate-in-charge, Robert Lubotsky.* Engineers: *Weisenger-Holland, Ltd.* (structural); *Wallace and Migdal, Inc.* (mechanical/electrical). Consultants: *John Geiner Designs* (graphics); *Robert Douglass* (store layouts). General contractor: *McCreary Construction Company.*

Philip Turner photos

The ducts, sprinklers and lights are all left exposed throughout the building (left); natural light enters through a band of windows placed high so that they allow a maximum amount of usable wall space, and also so that they are shielded from direct sunlight by the overhanging trusses. Large cloth banners in different colors (right) are hung in both the retail and warehouse sections, signalling where various items can be found.

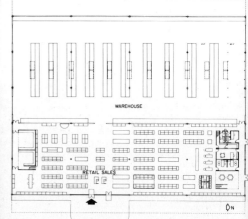

12

Housing the luxury merchandise of such national names as Cartier, Mark Cross, Georg Jensen and others, Kenton Center in Washington, D.C. accomplishes a twofold design goal. First, it establishes a contemporary vocabulary of elegance in background. Second, it provides opportunities for the individuality of each shop as a visible enclave in harmony with the background elegance. The simple expedient of costly materials for the background—white marble floor for the central court, cut velvet carpeting, polished stainless steel and bronze, wood paneling and fabrics for wall coverings—was supplementary to the design search for sophisticated contemporary ambiance. Shops are arranged along a white marble avenue approached through an arched tunnel entrance of molded stainless steel. Individual expression is provided by accents of change in color and materials within a disciplined palette. This permits the difference in identity between, say, Cartier and Jensen to be expressed without strident violation of the symphony. The emphasis at Cartier, for example, was on glass as a dominant material used for display cases on pedestals consistent with the dimensions of the jeweler's merchandise. Similarly, natural finished oak was the dominant material as background for the furniture of the Jensen shop, while a background of fabric materials provided backdrop for Mark Cross merchandise.

KENTON CENTER, Washington, D.C. Architects: *Copeland Novak and Israel—associate-in-charge, Edward C. Hambrecht.* Engineers: *S. W. Barbanel and Associates* (mechanical/electrical). Consultant: *Jules G. Horton Lighting Design, Inc.* Cabinetwork: *Anton Waldman Associates.* Contractor: *Edward M. Crough, Inc.*

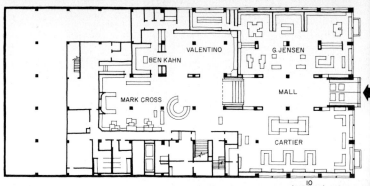

Arched entrances and stepped approaches to the marble avenue of stores at the Kenton Center are shown. The change of level at the center is shown at left flanked by Cartier and Jensen store entrances. The floating island motif repeated with a change in vocabulary from store to store is exemplified in the Mark Cross interior above.

69

3
Banks and
Branch Banks

Banks, and especially branch banks, continue to be built at ever-increasing rates—despite any adverse effect of economic cycles on other building types. The great number of branch banks are being built partially because of their newly realized profitability, and partially because of the changes in some states' laws, which have only recently allowed them. Accordingly, many of the banks shown in this chapter are relatively small branches.

All of the banks shown here illustrate one overriding principle: good design is an important key to attracting customers. Like images for stores and shops, images for banks carry a special message about the business transacted. But a bank's message is more serious. If it is either too flippant or too conservative, it will not tell customers what they want to know: that their bank is progressive and is—at the same time—taking the best possible care of their money.

And fortunately, many bank presidents and building committees have been astute enough to use architects and commission the best design as well as use interior designers when the architect does not carry out the interior work or graphics. The buildings on the following pages are all well designed within the context of their location and the type of clientele that is to be attracted. And the very sensible concept of the reuse of existing facilities is not forgotten in the examples. Accordingly, they are interestingly diverse.

Part of the diversity is due to an interesting phenomenon—regional style. Whenever the issue of regional style in architectural design is raised, it can quickly become the source of controversy both among architects and among clients who may be sensitive to a feared brand of provincialism. Still, the recognition of existing surroundings and localized construction methods (coupled with differing regional background influences) is going to produce some important and appropriate variations—whether created purposely or not. And it may be surprising to see that one of the largest degrees of regional variation can now be found in banks, once the most conformist of image-conscious building types.

Many of the banks shown here are located in different parts of the country, designed by local architects unafraid—as were their clients—to express (intuitively or purposely) a strong sense of where they are. The resulting diversity shows an increasingly better and more confident sense of the uniqueness of location than perhaps at any time since architecture took over local craftsmen's efforts—and it is certainly to be applauded in the face of much of the "sameness" that went before. It has been pointed out that the recent proliferation of smaller banks and branches is meant to bring business geographically "closer to home." Here it will be illustrated that these businesses are now not only closer to home; they can look like it.

1

Many new branch banks are by the sides of major highways in suburban and rural areas, on sites often connected with shopping centers. And that is the location for this 3,000-square-foot prototype near Memphis by architects Gassner/Nathan/Browne. There are currently six branches of approximately the same design under construction for this client, who originally commissioned the architects to design their headquarters downtown. All of C&I's new buildings reflect a conscious effort by an established bank to project a fresh appearance of vitality—a policy which has at least contributed to doubled deposits since the current construction program began.

Beside the obvious advantages of using a prototype (the prefabricated-steel roof-trusses can be ordered by phone), the repetitive appearance helps to establish an easily recognized identity on a type of site which can often lead to visual confusion. The building shape is simple and unobtrusive. The materials are distinctive rather than lavish. The poured-concrete walls and yellow-painted trusses duplicate elements of the headquarters building. Perforated aluminum panels have been applied to the underside of the metal roof-deck and are part of a straightforward over-all treatment. The construction cost was very low for this prototype which is the larger of two alternatives. The prototype concept has both cost and image advantages.

COMMERCIAL AND INDUSTRIAL BANK, Memphis, Tennessee. Architects: *Gassner/Nathan/Browne*. Engineers: *Kenworthy and Associates* (structural): *Griffith C. Burr* (electrical). Landscape architects: *Robert Green and Associates, Inc.* General contractor: *Claude R. Irwin.*

The bright-red and white logo of C&I was designed by the architects and is applied in a porcelain-enamel finish to the steel panels on the front of this prototype. Elsewhere, it is used by the bank on stationery and advertising. These colors contrast with the yellow paint on the roof trusses and the natural finish of the concrete walls at the sides and rear. Aluminum tiles supply a reflective glitter for the rear wall of the banking room.

Otto Baitz photos

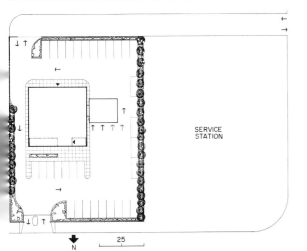

SERVICE STATION

N   25

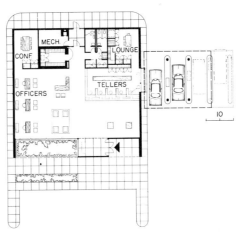

CONF   MECH.   LOUNGE

OFFICERS   TELLERS

10

2

This 4,300-square-foot bank was conceived by architects Marquis and Stoller as a box into which particular functions are cut without destroying the basic shape. The resulting unified form achieves identity by contrast to the more complicated facades of an adjacent shopping center and to the surrounding eucalyptus trees which were conscientiously preserved. It also allowed construction at a low cost.

Despite a seemingly simple shape, this building is not a prototype—as its planning and appearance involves a number of considerations particular to the site. A 15-foot height limitation was caused by proximity to an airport. The depth of each roof overhang has been determined by sun studies, and a skylight has been located to provide the inside with a maximum amount of natural light.

A local design review board would not approve the exposure of the steel structure which was required to bring the construction costs within the final very low amount. The resulting cement-plaster finish expresses the form of the building and is applied to metal studs which form the in-fill walls. The architects were requested to work with the client's own interior design consultants, MLTW/Turnbull, and they describe their collaboration as a happy one.

GOLDEN WEST SAVINGS, San Jose, California. Architects: *Marquis and Stoller—project architects: Janis Ong and Jon Winkelstein.* Engineers: *Forell/Elsesser* (structural); *Montgomery & Roberts* (mechanical); *Tage Hansen* (electrical). Interior design architects: *MLTW/ Turnbull Associates.* General contractor: *Harrod & Williams, Inc.*

Philip L. Molten photos

The white surfaces of furniture, which are standardized for all branches of Golden West, achieve a yellow glow from the color of the vertical surfaces under the skylight (left). The same color is used to emphasize the nature of the wall of the drive-through which is cut into the white surfaces of the building's box-like form. New proprietory window-mullions have a one inch face and visually reinforce the contrast between glass and solid wall areas by their "non-presence." Signage is also a client standard.

3

Located on a major highway near Knoxville, Tennessee, the site of this 4000-square-foot bank separates a shopping center from a residential area of single-family houses. As in the case of the similarly located buildings in this series, Hamilton relies on one forceful building shape to resolve the problems of identification in a confused environment. But here, the building shape is divided into the articulated elements of a predominant roof (defined by a precast-concrete fascia, into which the bank logo is recessed), massive non-structural piers of brick at the corners (above which the roof appears to float and which continue the shape of the roof), and a brick podium. All other elements are out of sight in deference to the clearness of a visual statement. The solid walls of the storage and utility spaces and a community room (an example of a new gesture of public welcome that is increasingly popular) are contained below the main banking level within the podium (access is gained by exterior stairs when the bank is closed). The air-conditioning condenser is below grade in a grate-covered pit. The main areas of banking room and drive-through teller locations are contained within the thusly unified building-shape as in an open pavilion. The project was the winner of an award from the Tennessee Society of Architects.

HAMILTON NATIONAL BANK, Knoxville, Tennessee. Architect: *McCarty Bullock Church Holsaple—designer: Robert Church, III; project manager: Charles Smith.* Engineers: *Scientific Methods Group* (structural); *Kurzynske and Associates* (mechanical). Landscape architect: *Melvin Kersey.* General contractor: *Rentenbach Engineering Co.*

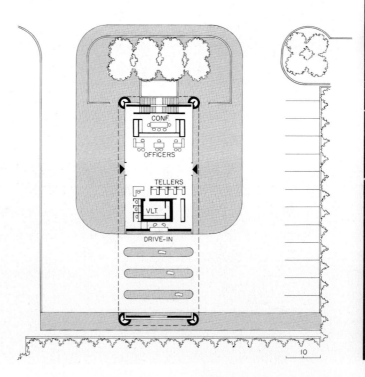

Elegance is carried through in the detailing and structure. This building is the only one in this series to show its steel frame. The four structural columns are welded plates, of a Y section, which are exposed within the brick piers. Air conditioning is accommodated through ceiling slots and base-board reveals, and the wood-strip covered walls. The few mullions are polished stainless steel (much of the glass is butted and doors are tempered glass). The banking-room floor is slate.

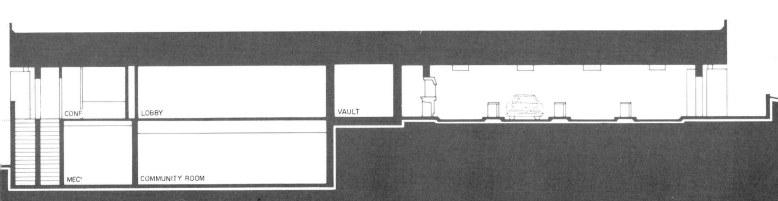

CONF   LOBBY   VAULT

MEC'   COMMUNITY ROOM

4

This is another branch bank that is located in a downtown area—a 9000-square-foot building in the densely populated Borough of Queens, New York City, by architect Edward Larrabee Barnes. Here, the site is almost fully occupied by a steel structure. The architect has deliberately used his typically flat planes of brick and glass cladding (in which the exterior surfaces of transparent and opaque materials are aligned) as a contrast to the "busy" treatments of the facades of the commercial buildings which are adjacent. For the users, the location of the glazing emphasizes a skyward view on one facade and indicates the location of the entry on the other. The smaller windows at street level offer confined areas for the usual bank advertising. The homogeneity of building surfaces is carried through with brick paving which covers the sidewalk and banking room alike and tends to invite the pedestrian inside by eliminating part of the psychological separation between the two areas. While the entry wall is pulled back from the line of adjacent facades to provide emphasis and some feeling of openness in this congested location, its end is sharply angled out toward the street-corner to avoid the incomplete line of adjacent building facades that would otherwise result. This also emphasizes the flat-plane design.

THE AMERICAN SAVINGS BANK, New York, New York. Architect: *Edward Larrabee Barnes*—associate-in-charge: *John Lee*; project architect: *Demetri Sarantitis*. Engineers: *Le Messurier Associates* (structural); *Pavane and Zuckermay* (mechanical/electrical). Consultants: *John Saladino* (interiors); *Chermayeff and Geismar* (graphics). General contractor: *A. J. Contracting, Inc.*

Nathanial Lieberman photos

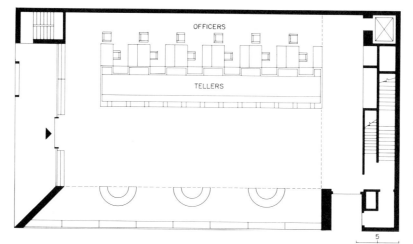

OFFICERS

TELLERS

5

Located on a congested urban street corner, this bank forms a quiet oasis of subdued materials treated in a homogeneous fashion. The main banking room, whose brick paving continues out to the curb, occupies almost all of the portion of the building above grade. Vault, employee lounge facilities (including a cheerful cafeteria) and other ancillary functions are located in a basement. There is a concerted effort here to reinforce and not compete with the scale of the surrounding buildings.

5

The original bank is a valuable part of the architectural heritage of the town of Andover, Massachusetts, a community of over twenty-five thousand people. It is prominently located on Main Street. As the number of the bank's customers and the range and type of its services began to outgrow the original facility, the bank was faced with the problem of remodeling with an addition, or constructing a completely new building.

The bank's managers elected to keep their beautifully detailed old building and to construct an addition to house new executive suites, conference rooms, lending officers' areas accessible to the public area and clerical staff space. The older building was to be generally remodeled, but its fine detailing was to be kept intact.

The neo-classic structure is symmetrical about both its longitudinal and transverse axes. The architects reoriented the major space circulation patterns from east to west to north and south. The tellers' counters were moved to the south wall (see isometric, opposite page top). They face three arched openings (opposite page bottom) which were once three arched windows in the north wall of the old bank.

Beyond, in the new double-height space, the drum staircase penetrates the new roof to become a source of daylight as can be seen in the section (right). By its form and position it serves as a focal element for the new spaces around it. The original north elevation has become a gateway to the new glazed double-height space, creating a dramatic juxtaposition between the new and the old. The addition is of steel-framed construction with masonry infill. At the main banking level is a slab on grade. The mezzanine and mechanical level floors are of concrete. The interior partitions are of metal stud or block. Surfaces are white painted plaster or drywall. Natural finish wood is used on the railing caps, window stools, tellers' counters, and the safe deposit vault screen.

The heating system was replaced and a new energy conserving air conditioning system was installed. All the interiors were designed by the architects. The cost of the remodeling, the addition and the interior furnishing was well below that of new construction.

ANDOVER SAVINGS BANK ADDITION, Andover, Massachusetts. Architects: *Shepley Bulfinch Richardson & Abbott*. Engineers: *Abraham Woolf* (structural); *Shoosuanian Engineering Associates* (mechanical); *Lotero & Mason* (electrical). General contractor: *Charles Construction Company*.

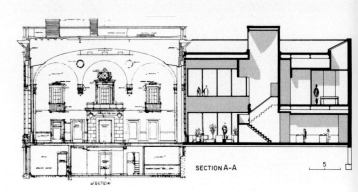

SECTION A-A

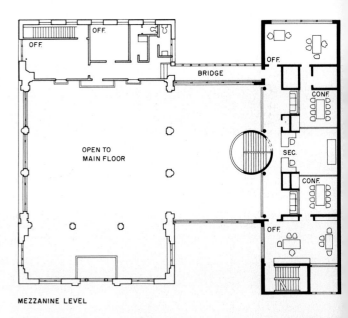

MEZZANINE LEVEL

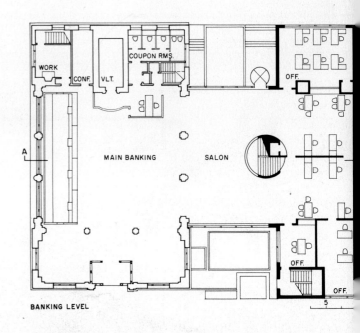

BANKING LEVEL

As the isometric (right) indicates, the addition is spare and simple in its expression and is without ornamentation. It relates to the older wing by means of its symmetry and by its shared wall. Its restraint acts as a foil for the rich decoration of the older banking room. At the same time, the new space has a spatial vitality of its own.

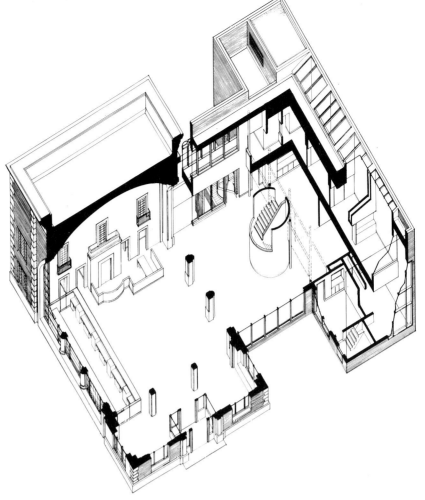

Ron Levenson

6

As opposed to a large banking house, local branches of public-service banks attract accounts, in no small part, by the image which they present to potential "retail" customers. Hanover National Bank and architects Bohlin and Powell gambled on an image, for this Kingston, Pa. branch, which hardly asserts itself at all. Happily, its commercial success has exceeded original expectations—perhaps out of public appreciation of the owner's consideration.

Facing a main street which is partially residential, and a side street lined with large older houses, the building is almost difficult to see—its faceted, mirrored glass facade will eventually reflect only wisteria and trumpet and grape vines, currently in early growth on a wood arbor along the streets. Besides providing a foil for the mirrored glass, the trellises shade pedestrians, provide an edge for the semi-urban site and—from within—visually expand the space of the banking room. "The last thing that corner needed was another disruptive building of the type that is destroying the scale and flavor of cohesive towns," says Peter Bohlin.

Like the offices for Westinghouse by the same architects (see index), this unusual building is "special" only where it needs to be: on the street sides. The concept is really that of

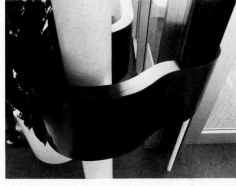

an inexpensive masonry and steel-frame box cut away only where it counts, and to expand the handsome "front lawn." The construction is typical of light commercial structures. The angled windows are set in standard "store front" aluminum framing.

The partitioned spaces are arranged along the rectangular walls in no formal arrangement but "just where they want to be". The vault is located for easy access to the tellers, one of whom can double at an interior station and the drive-up counter. Drywall-partitioned offices for the officers are adjacent to the waiting area. A block of service spaces is between the offices and vault, and includes a stair to an employees' lounge on the floor below.

Bohlin sees even more valuable application of this "non-building" concept for large projects, which can be even more disruptive in established areas, and he intends to try it again. As for the solid rear walls: "We'll just wait for the ivy to grow."

HANOVER NATIONAL BANK BRANCH, Kingston, Pa. Architects: *Bohlin and Powell*—partner-in-charge: *Richard E. Powell*; project architect: *Don Maxwell*. Engineers: *Vincent B. Szykman, Inc.* (structural); *Martin and Fladd* (mechanical/electrical). General contractor: *Sordoni Construction Co.*

Jon Jackson, Russell Roberts photos

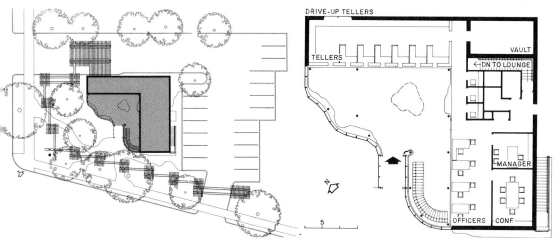

As planted wisteria and grapes grow over the wood trellises, the building will increasingly disappear. By contrast, the interior is brightly colored and crisply detailed. The red surfaces of the tellers' counter (opposite page, bottom) continue around the room as a writing surface and a back rest for a brilliant green couch in the waiting area (see plan) designed by the architects. A "free form" opening was cut through the standard acoustical ceiling for the skylight, and reveals the exposed steel structure which has been painted a soft gray. Hanging pots of Swedish ivy become the "chandeliers" and light diffuser.

7

According to Pontchartrain president Edward Boldt, deposits equalled almost four times the original capitalization in the first 15 months of this bank's existence. Part of this success is due to a previously untapped market—in the midst of gas stations and drive-in theaters outside of New Orleans. Part is credited to market research—which suggested the large number of drive-in tellers. Apparently, the research indicated no prejudice against banking in a recycled night clug—which the building is (photo, right).

The dominant view from the highway, of the wood trussed, steel sheathed roofs over each teller station was the result of architects Caldwell & Turchi's making an asset out of the inability to place the stations more conventionally on the restricted site (see plan). The roofs were given their distinctive shape which made a strong identification for the building, and have—in no little way—increased the success of the public appeal. The only other major additions to the inherited "box" were a larger complementary roof over the entrance (photo, right), an adjacent gallery providing covered passage from the parking area, and low walls around the site perimeter. Besides providing an ideal surface for painting the repeated name of the bank for the benefit of speeding cars, the

walls contain the site in a tight way, and give it identity in its confusing environment.

The decision to reuse an existing building was made in 1973 when New Orleans was in a construction boom and labor and materials were scarce, causing long delays on new structures. As the bank was anxious for a speedy opening, reuse made the most sense then—as it may now when the greater costs of new construction become deciding factors. Although not primarily concerned with budget, the clients obtained their new space for an extremely low cost. This included a new mechanical system, interior finishes, added structure and new facing consisting of painted-concrete sewer bricks on metal stud backup—the only practical and readily available material at the time. The white dry-wall partitions within are enlivened with bright color and an additional wall of brick at the vaults.

PONTCHARTRAIN STATE BANK, Metairie, Louisiana. Architects: *Caldwell & Turchi*—partner-in-charge: *Nano J. Turchi, Jr.* Engineers: *Arnold R. Smythe, Jr.* (structural); *Goldstein & Goldstein, Inc.* (mechanical); *Ohlsen & Mitchell, Inc.* (electrical). Consultants: *Louisiana Interiors* (interiors); *Nationwide Building Consultants, Inc.* (banking). Contractors: *Goliath Construction Co.* (general); *Bayou Fabricators and Erectors* (structural steel)

C. F. Weber photos

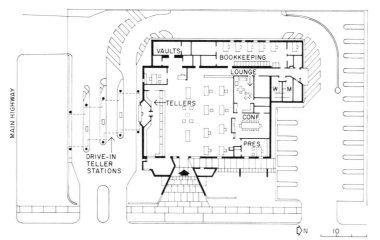

Because of a narrow site, the drive-in tellers' stations wound up—unconventionally—on the front of the building and were turned into an identifying asset (photos, below) by emphasis on their form and structure: wood trusses and oversized pipe columns. Most of the other modifications to the original structure (top photo, opposite) were achieved by resurfacing the exterior, and with paint. The interiors, with bright, boldly colored furniture, reflect the "up and coming" attitude that the bank promotes. Part of the roadside environment, a drive-in movie screen, can be seen in the photo below.

8

Paul Kivett photos

Abend Singleton Associates made free use of mirrors that reflect the images of street activity and animate this small Midwestern banking interior. These mirrors, combined with a serpentine glazing line installed without mullions on the street facade, provide a pleasant spatial ambiguity—an ambiguity that detaches the banking space visually from the strict rectilinear geometry of the existing building form. An appropriate personal design note is the use of an old vault door, covered in glass, to create a check writing table. Wood and oak contrast effectively.

MERCANTILE BANK, Kansas City, Missouri, Architects: *Abend Singleton Associates.* Engineers: *Bob D. Campbell & Co.* (structural); *Associated Engineering Consultants, Inc.* (mechanical). Contractor: *D. F. Cahill Construction Co.*

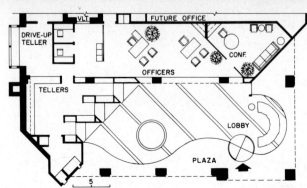

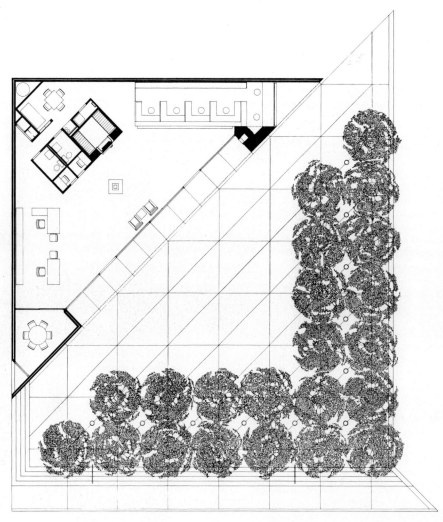

Gerald Allen photos

9

Tom Walters

Built on a corner lot along a busy commercial strip in a low-income neighborhood, this branch bank turns inward, away from the passing vehicular scene, to its own plaza shaded by a grove of plane trees. The shape of the building and the configuration of the site (see plan, opposite) were not, in spite of all appearances, products of the availability of 45-degree triangles in the drafting room. Instead, they reflect a pre-existing path across the site made by children on their way to and from school. Now they take their short cut across the plaza (above right).

Perhaps the act of presenting a street with blank, brick walls is rather anti-social. In our own country it is often regarded as such, though in Latin cultures it causes little rancor. In this case, what is lost by the act needs to be balanced against what is gained by the creation of the quiet plaza behind.

BEATTIES FORD ROAD BRANCH, NORTH CAROLINA NATIONAL BANK, Charlotte, North Carolina. Architects: *Wolf Associates*. Engineers: *R. V. Wasdell Associates* (structural); *Mechanical Engineers, Inc.* (mechanical); *John Bolen Consulting Engineers* (electrical). General Contractor: *Butler and Sidbury, Inc.*

Joshua Freiwald photos

The Manzano branch is located next to a shopping center. Views toward the distant mountains are limited by surrounding commercial development and hence by limited fenestration. The solid volume of the building has walls that are parallel to the roads at the entrance and at the drive-in teller positions. A changing decorative element is created by the shadows of surrounding trees on the precast and poured concrete walls.

10-11-12

Perhaps the most determined of the architects here in a search for a regional vernacular, Antoine Predock has evolved highly individual imagery in his designs for these branches of The First National Bank in Albuquerque. He sees this imagery as more of a response to environmental considerations than to a stylistic recall of indigenous architecture, although the allusion is clearly evident.

In the case of the three branches shown here, each occupies a location in a different roadside commercial area of varying appeal for the extremes of varying income groups. And each has different problems of relating to views, wind, sun—and, of course, the public. But the three share common materials such as warmly-colored, bushed-hammered concrete walls and—perhaps more importantly a certain ruggedness which speaks distinctly of the hearty Southwest. Each of the branches is essentially triangular in plan. In the case of the two on this and the opposite page, the roof—like a sheltering hat—slopes down toward the southern corner, a prow into sandstorms and the heat of mid-day. On the opposite "open" side of the building, the treatments are very different. At Manzano, the tellers occupy this focal position in a low projection from the main room, and a clerestory over them is the main source of the natural light and limits views of the pervasively commercial surroundings. The higher-ceilinged main room is devoted to a large space required by the particular program for a large banking consultation area. Roof-top mechanical equipment is concealed by high parapet walls. The steel structure is clad in sandblasted precast-concrete panels, while the vault is constructed of contrasting poured-in-place concrete. The exposed walls of the vault are carefully articulated from the panels (photo above).

At Sandia Plaza, the open side of the triangular plan is literally open through glass walls to a court, paved with quarry tile which continues into the banking room and onto the sloping roofs. The expansive views visually extend the banking room and include distant mountains above a planted berm in the court. The berm largely conceals the low-lying commercial development of the surrounding regional center. The diagonal through the site made by the building provides a convenient path for pedestrians to other locations within the center. The entire building's structure and enclosing walls are poured-in-place concrete. The walls are sandblasted, and the roof is a post-tensioned "waffle" slab in which recessed lighting brightens an ambiance that feels open to the outside. Two other interesting projects shown overleaf illustrate Predock's versatility with different programs and the purposefulness in his designs.

BRANCHES OF THE FIRST NATIONAL BANK IN ALBUQUERQUE, Albuquerque, New Mexico. Architect: *Antoine Predock*. Engineers: *Randy Holt* (structural, Manzano); *Robert Krause* (structural, Sandia Plaza); *Allison Engineering* (mechanical); *Don Fowler* (electrical). General contractors: *Bellamah Corporation* (Manzano); *Lembke Construction* (Sandia Plaza).

The Sandia Plaza branch has exterior walls that—like Manzano—are parallel to surrounding roadways, which are connected to an adjacent shopping center. However, here the resulting rectangular volume has been cut away to provide a walled court, shielded from the streets in a locally traditional fashion (photo, right) and extending the sense of space from within. Earth berms, planted with local materials, and a fountain create a quiet oasis within the walls.

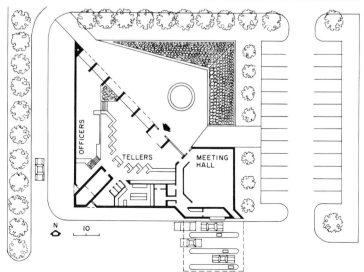

Joshua Freiwald photos

The West Central Branch is located in the most visually and economically deprived area of the three. Accordingly, it has its own pleasant interior environment with minimal windows. The angled entrance is designed to fit in the juncture of the existing building and a future wing. The latter will help to contain the entrance plaza (photo, left). To contribute a positive element to the environment, the building is located on a large lawn, which extends down an adjacent hill and covers a screening berm to the east, where distant views of mountains are thus framed.

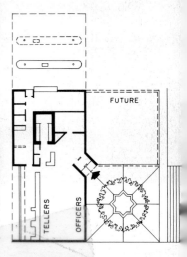

Other projects for the First National Bank by Predock include a remodeling of the downtown headquarters which the architect described as a previously badly abused neoclassic building. In a shift from his design for all new buildings, he has restored the building to its former character. At the other end of the spectrum are steel frame mobile branches, which can be pulled from temporary site to temporary site on wheels. The wheels are sunken below grade during the unit's stay in one place. These units are expected to be replaced by the construction of permanent branches. The steel framing and decking is exposed on the interior.

Gil Amiaga photos

13

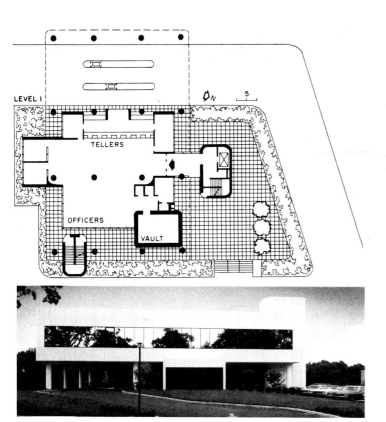

LEVEL I

TELLERS

OFFICERS

VAULT

Alluding to the Villa Savoye, architects Michael Harris Spector & Associates state that the Bank of Suffolk County makes no pretense of assimilating into its environment—the V-shaped intersection of two major highways. Like the Villa, it appears as a machine—but for banking instead of living. Accordingly, it is a visual extension of the much larger man-made environment of nearby New York City and—at the same time—complements by the contrast of its stark-white, porcelain-finished metal panels the surroundings of dark greenery and paving. It also projects its surroundings to passers-by through reflective-glass windows, which are gasketed into, and are flush with, the panels. Unlike those of other projects shown in this chapter, this bank's designers and owners clearly believe that the building itself should be highly visible to the public. Like those projects, this is a well thought-out response to environmental conditioning.

The building's sculptural quality is achieved by verticality in predominantly flat surroundings and by an arrangement of elements that are composed for equal interest from any view. The banking floor is freely defined by a number of enclosed forms containing specific functions such as the vault and stairs, and it is capped by a rectangular floor of flexibly planned offices. Drive-in teller windows are located within the building.

CORPORATE HEADQUARTERS, BANK OF SUFFOLK COUNTY, Hauppauge, New York. Architects: *Michael Harris Spector & Associates*. Engineers: *Thompson & Czark* (structural); *S. Limoggio & Associates* (mechanical/electrical). General contractor: *Abraham Shames*.

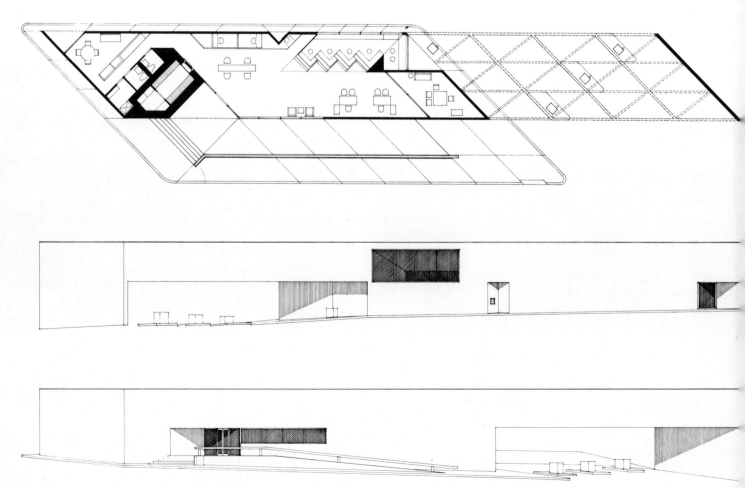

Gordon Schenck

Gerald Allen

14

Gordon Schenck

Gerald Allen

The design of this suburban branch bank reflects the owner's predictions that as many as 80 per cent of all banking transactions would take place from drive-in teller positions. Accordingly, the automobile lanes carved out of the volume of the building and served by a system of pneumatic tubes make this, literally, a drive-in bank.

The steeply sloping site (a major consideration) is on a main artery between two major shopping centers and several large office buildings. Diagonal movement across the site — and thus the shape of the building itself — results from the fact that the main entrance is at the lower southeastern corner and the exit, as well as a secondary entrance, is at the upper northeastern corner. This configuration also preserves the large, handsome trees in the northeastern corner of the site.

The bank is built very economically of steel columns and joists, wood studs, and plywood sheathing painted white. Its long flat side faces the street, and announces itself with an assertive elegance to passing cars.

A large parking lot in front of the building accommodates the cars of employees and also of customers whose business is too extensive to be

transacted from the drive-in teller positions. Inside the building, in a space ingeniously configured and lit by high north windows, are tellers, a conference room, and coupon booths.

PARK ROAD BRANCH, NORTH CAROLINA NATIONAL BANK, Charlotte, North Carolina. Architects: *Wolf Associates*. Engineers: *R. V. Wasdell Associates* (structural); *Mechanical Engineers, Inc.* (mechanical); *Connor Bullard Associates* (electrical). General contractor: *Rodgers Builders, Inc.*

15

Until recently, the international financing and investment operations of the J. Henry Schroder Banking Corporation were conducted on the upper floors of a 40-story building in Manhattan's financial center. With this new design, parts of those operations have been brought down to the street level and housed in a way that strongly declares to the public a "solid" image and a respect for quality—particularly appropriate for the responsibilities of diversified financial management in some 14 countries and Hong Kong.

Initially, the bank's intent was simply to consolidate operations in a more efficient manner in space previously unused, and—at the same time—free areas in the upper stories for sub-rental. But Ferguson Sorrentino Design Inc.—working with several members of the client firm assigned full-time to the project—created this much bolder solution. It includes the semi-public main area for client consultation (photo, opposite page), the small retail banking area (top, right) placed on the ground floor, a new mezzanine inserted to complete the semi-public program, and the location of related executives on a remodeled part of the floor above (photo, below).

The design was accomplished within the constraints of typical, commercial-office space. Part of the main banking room's substantial character is achieved by unusually high ceilings, accomplished by "squeezing up" the typical horizontal mechanical transfers that occur above the ground floors of such high-rises. An even-more-important result of raising the "building-standard" ceiling to 18 feet was the ability to provide a mezzanine, without which the program could not have been met within the available floor area. But the most difficult innovation was tying the usually isolated (because of the transfers) ground and second floors together visually and functionally. This was accomplished by a stair snaked around the building's electrical distribution box (photo, right). Continuous recessed lighting isolates the stair's surfaces from those adjacent and leads the viewer from level to level. The resulting effect achieves a connection between floors at relatively low cost—but with high impact. It also provides the bank with a built-in sculpture.

J. HENRY SCHRODER BANKING CORPORATION, New York, New York. Designers: *Ferguson Sorrentino Design, Inc.—project manager: Lee Manners; job captain: David Light; assistant: Archibald Johnson.* Engineers: *James Ruderman* (structural); *M. A. DiGiacomo Associates* (mechanical). General contractor: *Arnott-Bennis, Inc.*

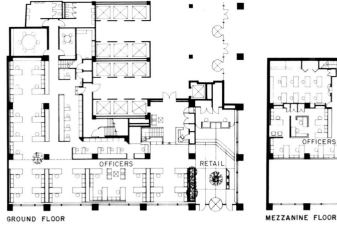

GROUND FLOOR

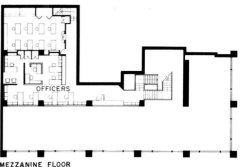

MEZZANINE FLOOR

The desks and seating in the ground-floor client-consultation space (photo, below) are supported by a series of parallel carpeted platforms which provide separation between officers, acoustical privacy, and contain electric and telephone lines. The resulting arrangement allows for an intimate and luxurious atmosphere (despite the partitionless plan), which is enhanced by natural materials of wood and leather. Despite the use of a "building standard" ceiling, careful attention to lighting includes different lamp types for various locations, new recessed incandescents and the spectacular panels over the main room.

16

The present impact of this bank interior belies the routine, awkward shopping center stall with which the architects began. Moore Grover Harper, P.C. (formerly Charles W. Moore Associates), in designing this branch of the County Federal Savings and Loan Association, accepted the tunnel-like space, but enriched it with an illusion of flexure, and vivid colors.

The banking room is divided across the narrow dimension by parallel partitions (see plan) into which are cut irregular openings. Taken together—visually superimposed—the openings appear in graceful rotation as one looks toward the mirrored rear wall of the room. Single six-foot, warm-white fluorescent tubes with integral ballasts provide general illumination and further the effect of the partitions.

The corner space includes windows fronting on a main thoroughfare. Through the windows, nighttime passers-by glimpse a giant neon star, the bank's logo, which is repeated in specially cut vinyl floor tile in red and and white. This contrasts to the royal blue carpeting surrounding it, and the red ceiling above.

Architects: *Moore Grover Harper, P.C.* Interiors: *Moore Grover Harper, P.C. and Mary Ann Rumney.* Associate architect: *Richard Oliver.* Lighting: *Moore Grover Harper, P.C.* Graphics consultant: *Mary Ann Rumney.* Contractor: *Gene Schmid.*

Robert Perron photos

CONF.

BANKING

LOBBY

17

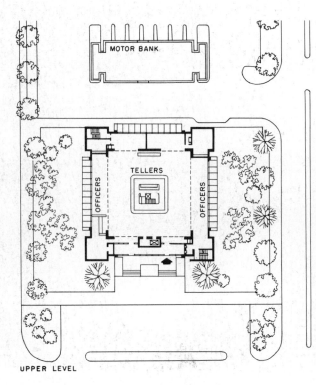

MOTOR BANK

OFFICERS — TELLERS — OFFICERS

UPPER LEVEL

Far from the wide open plains but recalling them in its strong horizontality, the Northpark National Bank occupies a corner of the site of the innovative Northpark Shopping Center (innovative because of its double-level plan) in suburban Dallas. Designed by the Omniplan architects (who were also responsible for Northpark), the relatively small bank's purposely strong proportions and white brick cladding are intended to achieve an additional objective to that of complementing the Center's forceful horizontality. They are also intended to visually assert the bank's importance, which could have been easily overwhelmed by the massive neighbor.

A large banking room on the steel-framed main level is designed to accommodate the demands of a planned additional three stories of banking facilities. A central teller's "island" has direct vertical access to the bookkeeping department on the concrete constructed floor below. The bank's interiors were designed by Mrs. E. G. Hamilton, wife of the Omniplan partner, and contain red carpeting and blue upholstered seating of unusually muted coloring. These furnishings are contrasted to white brick walls on which are hung a rotating display of artwork loaned by Raymond Nasher, the owner of Northpark and the chairman of the bank.

NORTHPARK NATIONAL BANK, Dallas, Texas. Architects: *Omniplan—principal-in-charge: E. G. Hamilton.* Engineers: *Datum Structures Engineering* (structural); *Raymond Goodson Jr., Inc.* (soils); *William Hall & Co.* (mechanical/electrical). Landscape architect: *Richard Vignola.* General contractor: *Henry C. Beck Company.*

Jeof Winningham

Michael Haynes

4
Office Buildings and Corporate Headquarters

It took until 1930 for the United States to accumulate a billion square feet of office space, while during the following three decades that number nearly doubled. So far, in the seventies, many million square feet of office space have been started, and according to the New York Regional Plan Association, the country will double its total office space again by the year 2000.

The offices on the following pages are part of this surge. They reflect, however, more than the accumulation of floor space; recurrent here are design qualities that reveal an increasingly sophisticated corporate client, and architectural thinking that departs from conventional office planning and design. Corporate image, expansion potential (very important), and human amenities are the key program requirements; more square footage per employee is common, often between 175 and 200 square feet; and the idea of the office as something dynamic is itself growing.

As a building type, the office building has always been of special interest to the architect first because its scope is well within the capabilities of any design office, large or small, and second because of the challenge of finding the particular expression which, if corporate, best represents the client, or, if speculative, will best attract tenants

Despite the many thousands of office buildings that have been built, the special requirements of each project present opportunities for imaginative handling of known factors and for inclusion of new ideas. How to achieve the flexibility of tenant use in a speculative building, for instance, is a constant challenge; so is the handling of on-site parking where it exists. If a few truly inventive solutions appear, there are nevertheless dozens of innovative approaches used which prove effective within their context.

The idea of renovating deteriorated older office buildings in lieu of all-new construction is gaining more popular acceptance because it has several advantages: lower costs, easier local acceptance, and the realization that older buildings — contrary to previous belief — can supply, through their inherent dignity, desirable corporate images. Several examples of interesting renovations appear here.

Another increasingly important issue in office building design is gaining the acceptance of such new construction by local planning boards and community groups, when the new construction is being proposed for either an area without similar precedent — or for one that may already appear too dense. Both of these situations are explored by the examples that follow.

1

There is a real problem of architectural conscience, or at least there *should* be, when a prospective client calls up and wants to discuss building a skyscraper smack-dab in the middle of an otherwise low-scale downtown. Back in 1967, when officials of the Worcester County National Bank in Massachusetts called up Roche Dinkeloo and Associates (doing so at the suggestion of J. Irwin Miller, the supporter of design excellence in Columbus, Indiana, for whom they had designed many buildings), Worcester's downtown was so low-scale that anything higher than its old city hall, on Harrington Corner, would have stood out. More than a decade having passed, communities no longer automatically regarded tall buildings as beneficial, mainly be-

cause so many of them, however carefully done, bring along an almost inherent truculence in trying to relate to the streets and buildings which already exist. The officials of a bank may want image, identity, and amenity. They may want a building that stands for their city's cultural and economic comeback. They may even want, as one official at Worcester says, "something more than pulling out a drawer and picking out an erector-set design." Still the problem of conscience persists for an architect. What is the response to be? Turn the job down? Or turn the problem around, designing, more than some stunning, symbolic slab, an example of decent, deferential manners? The Worcester County National Bank Building, as completed, a 24-story twin tower framed of steel and sheathed in mirrored glass, comes about as close to having good manners as this architectural genre can.

Known as Worcester Plaza, the building is at Pleasant and Main Streets just west of the granitic elegance of city hall and the spacious

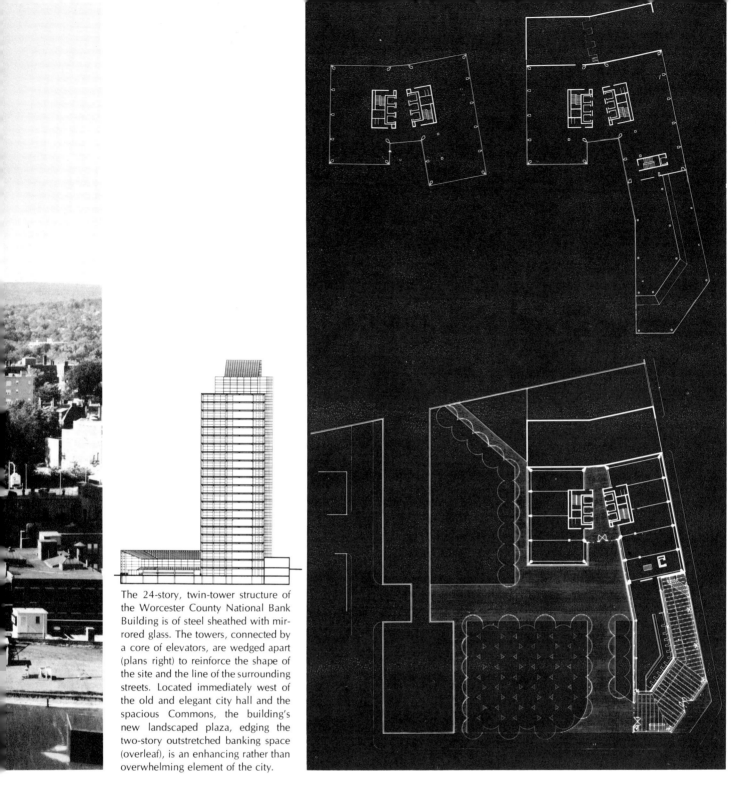

The 24-story, twin-tower structure of the Worcester County National Bank Building is of steel sheathed with mirrored glass. The towers, connected by a core of elevators, are wedged apart (plans right) to reinforce the shape of the site and the line of the surrounding streets. Located immediately west of the old and elegant city hall and the spacious Commons, the building's new landscaped plaza, edging the two-story outstretched banking space (overleaf), is an enhancing rather than overwhelming element of the city.

Common. Front Street reaches east from this junction, lined with shops, and linking up with the commerce and retail lined malls called Worcester Center. The Common has recently been spruced up by the landscape architectural firm of Sasaki, while the Center, a few years old, was done by Welton Becket, all of which was anticipated by Worcester Plaza. Its first design—a 46-story, poured-concrete tower rising from a vast greenhouse-style lobby area—was announced in 1969 to a public that went absolutely ga-ga and my-gosh and oh-no. "Assuring Worcester's prominence," so the bankers bleated, was the aim and, so several critics including Aline Saarinen suggested, it was one of Roche Dinkeloo's finest moments—albeit one that didn't last. The completed version, considerably scaled down from the earlier 400,000-square-feet to a more manageable and affordable 280,000— about half for the bank and the rest for renting out—is a much finer moment, even as restrictions of budget and marketplace potential were what impelled a more modestly scaled solution.

A primary consideration, as the new design evolved, was reinforcing the existing pattern of streets rather than, as in the earlier version, rising in majestic aloofness from them. The two towers, linked by a core of elevators and utilities, were angled away from each other at 11½ degrees. This wedging apart of what might have been a more routine rectilinear plan does several nice things. As the office towers pull away from each other, elevator lobbies are created and, being recessed between the two, show up as a vertical spine of space anchoring the shimmering facades. Another nice thing about the wedging is that the site, wedge-shaped itself, is thus enhanced. Finally, while the towers are set back from Main Street with a landscaped plaza in front, the two-level banking lobby with its mezzanine of offices overlooking the main space, edges down Pleasant Street, nudging the sidewalk, and then turns the corner at Main. This out-stretched arm grabs the

environment and is a natural horizontal extension of the towers' vertical thrust. Both are 50 feet wide. One is a hundred feet deep; the other, 80. These alternately recessing and assertive masses, with the indentation of the core, give the thrust texture and make the verticality less intrusive. It becomes less a building in the city and more a building of the city—a calm come-on.

This character is pointed up by the treatment of glass. The curtain walls are composed of three different color bands on each floor, and these have varied levels of reflectivity. This treatment contrasts with the clear glass which sheathes the core on both ends, allowing a see-through effect in viewing the building from outside. At the curtain wall of the office towers, the lightest band of glass is at eye level; the darkest, by the floor. Metal-covered neoprene gaskets hold the ten-foot-wide sheets; floor levels are denoted by the horizontal bands.

A sharply angled roof surmounts the core which becomes a two-

story lobby, ebulliently lit and finished with mirrored and stainless steel surfaces, and serves the shamelessly posh private club, bar and restaurant that take up the 23rd and 24th floors. The view from this top-side dining room to the city and its Seven Hills is arresting in its beauty as the cityscape stretches beyond to a striking horizon. Around sunset, the colors of the sky are strongly picked up by the reflective finishes and richly textured fabrics of the space. It is a thoroughly successful interior.

At ground level, the banking space picks up the external environment in a compelling fashion. Greenhouse-style, the roof of this two-level room, paved in earth-colored tiles, is of stippled glass. Over the tellers, protecting them from possible glare, stretches a trellis-like awning arrangement of metal and glass. The tone is rather that of a conservatory or a partially shaded sidewalk cafe. It is small-town, affable, pleasant—a truly urbane place. And there is not a hint of the

paste-on pretentiousness so often associated with banking or big business establishments.

Throughout the building, the twin-tower solution yields dividends. Just getting out of an elevator is delightful, looking out, as one can, to the city below. The towers, one of them 4,500 square feet and the other 3,500, accommodate six corner offices on each floor and two sizable reception areas—all with good views. And because the floor sizes are manageable, both large and small tenants can be flexibly taken care of. On the lower levels of the towers, a variety of retail and service shops have moved in, thus adding to the building's permeability and identification with the street-sauntering public. And from the fourth level, at the core, a bridge reaches out from the back of the building to a 600-car parking structure, thus consolidating and concealing the necessary if noxious presence of automobiles.

"Those are the circumstances," as John Dinkeloo suggests, "that make up what we do. We do not just design. We derive. And that is why a certain truth comes out, which it can't do if you high-pressure a situation and try to force yourself upon circumstances." Worcester Plaza tells the truth about a tough situation for any architect facing the problem of fitting into surroundings that, as at Worcester, needed to be beefed up rather than bludgeoned. In a moment of rare enthusiasm, Kevin Roche said of it, "The results are not unpleasant." With an enthusiasm as rare, when it comes to liking skyscrapers, the people in this old industrial town have taken to it as well. Telling, isn't it, how architectural conscience can raise that of everyone else?

WORCESTER COUNTY NATIONAL BANK, WORCESTER PLAZA, Worcester, Massachusetts. Owner: *Worcester County National Bank*. Architect: *Roche Dinkeloo and Associates*. Engineers: *Pfisterer Tor and Associates (structural); Hubbard Lawless and Osborne (electrical)*. Contractors: *Blount-Fontaine (general); E.A. Berman Co. (mechanical); Coghlin, Inc. (electrical)*.

The 23rd and 24th floors of the Worcester County National Bank Building are occupied by private restaurant and club spaces that are reached through a two-story lobby (top) of highly reflective surfaces of glass and mirror-finish stainless steel. The sharp angle of the roof surmounting the lobby is brightly lit, its slanting surfaces shimmering with a kaleidescopic effect. The layout, finishes, and fittings of the dining space are conceived to grasp a wide view of the stark horizon. Recessed lighting, carried in stainless steel continuous soffits below the ceiling, give the room a floating effect and soften the juncture between walls and ceiling, inside and out. Down to the last knife and fork, the interiors are among Roche and Dinkeloo's finest.

Ezra Stoller © ESTO photos

BANK OF TOKYO

2

In searching for a solution to outmoded facilities with a dated
appearance, Manhattan's Bank of Tokyo found what was,
for a commercial institution, a revolutionary new answer: stay
in the existing building, preserve its visual assets of a
grand facade and great public space, and replace
its inadequate functional areas with sparkling new facilities
—which give freshness to the whole project. Here is
an example of good vision by the designers,
good sense by the client, and good luck for the city.

Behind the "traditional" facade there is an almost-completely-new building, which is viewed first through a new recessed, ground-floor arcade (photo top). Within, the original central bay of the banking room has been surrounded by new construction. The central theme of the redesign is a sculpture by Isamu Noguchi.

Many critics have often discussed the desirability of preservation and re-use of older buildings—not just of maintaining examples of architects' past efforts, but to leave the valuable, varied context of the neighborhood intact. Too often, however, directors of corporations have thought that headquarters in older buildings were incompatible with the appearance of commercial efficiency, and they have moved from or torn down distinguished buildings primarily to obtain that desired "image." Thus. . . .

The newly remodeled Manhattan branch of the Bank of Tokyo is exceptional for two reasons. First, it clearly demonstrates that a sensitive remodeling—designed by Kajima International—can produce relatively inexpensive but prestigious "new" space with not only a progressive image, but a highly urbane and memorable image as well. Secondly, this project is distinguished in its respect for its environment: in its highly visible location across the street from the venerable Trinity Church Yard (foreground of bottom photo, previous page), the renovation has maintained the flavor of a uniquely "settled" neighborhood, and it has avoided the usual prolonged disruption of a new-construction site by producing the new space in a short time (during which—by planned staging—the tenants never left the building).

Essentially, Kajima's approach was to almost completely rebuild the interiors of 13 floors of the 22-floor building (designed by architect Bruce Price and built between 1894 and 1896) and to provide new glazing, elevators and mechanical systems for the remaining floors. Left intact, of course, was the structural frame,

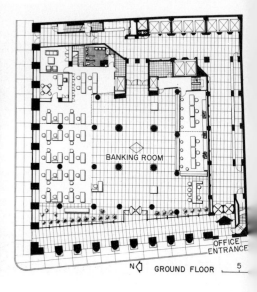

BANKING ROOM

OFFICE ENTRANCE

N GROUND FLOOR 5

the irreplaceable ornamented central bay of the banking room, the ceiling of the elevator lobby, and the elaborately carved stone facade. The crisp design of the new construction surrounding the central bay and on the floors above was designed in deliberate contrast to the richness and elaborations of the remaining original detail. And to accommodate and welcome the public at large, the frameless ground-floor glazing facing Trinity Church was pulled back to produce an inviting open arcade and a completely "modern" facade behind the original.

The design of the upper floors of the original building had largely been ignored in the original construction, and resembled the characterless spaces in many commercial buildings of the same vintage. Here, everything is new and appropriately appears that way. Each floor is entered via large elevator lobbies and reception areas, which provide an up-to-date spaciousness. New bronze-glass and metal window units are set in splayed recesses to reflect the natural light, while accommodating the two-foot wall thickness of the old facades.

The designers have produced "a journey forward in time." The elevator lobby for the main floor (photo, above) is a white marble "funnel" leading through the original space to the starkly contemporary interiors on the floors above (photo, below).

THE BANK OF TOKYO, New York City. Client: The Bank of Tokyo. Designers: *Kajima International, Inc.— Nobutaka Ashihara, director; Ryozo Iwashiro, project designer; Martin Frauwirth, manager.* Associated architects: *Welton Becket Associates— Charles Ginste, project director.* Owner: *Sylvan Lawrence Company, Inc.—Fred Safran, architect to the owner.* Engineers: *Welton Becket Associates* (structural); *Lehr Associates* (mechanical/electrical). Consultants: *Donald Bliss* (lighting); *Carlos Ramirez & Albert Woods, Inc.* (graphics); *Frank N. Giampietro Associates Inc.* (kitchen); *Jerome Menell Company, Inc.* (audio-visual). General contractor: *Safran Builders, Inc.*

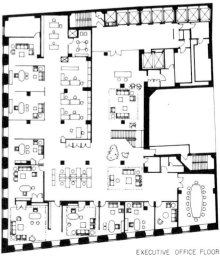

EXECUTIVE OFFICE FLOOR

3

Citizens Bank Center in Richardson, Texas (a Dallas suburb), meets a complex series of program requirements in a structure of stunning simplicity and visual strength. Designed by OMNIPLAN Architects Harrell + Hamilton with Datum Structures Engineering, Inc., the 13-story office building stands above 35,000 square feet of banking space and 15,000 square feet of retail space. The designers have created for the bank the desired strong identity with a form that instantly says "something special" even to the uninitiated.

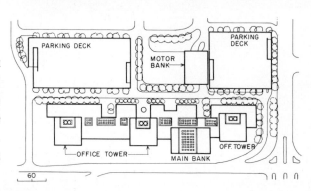

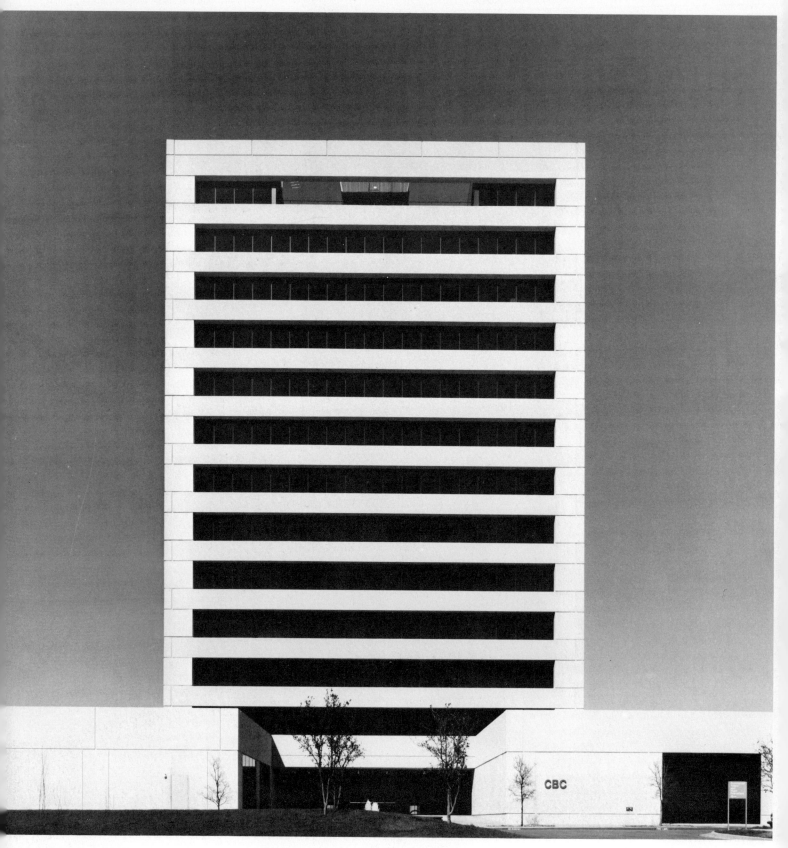

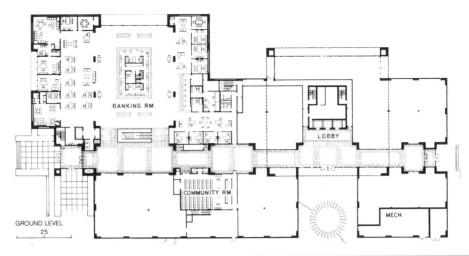

BANKING RM.

LOBBY

COMMUNITY RM.

MECH.

GROUND LEVEL
25

The structure is a hybrid: the cage is precast, the core was slip-formed, and the floor is steel

The program for Citizens Bank Center called for a strong visual identity, a form that would attract attention by motorists passing on the expressway. It also asked for an image that would express the bank's commitment to long-term ownership. Yet it wanted a building that would be suitable to what is a more suburban than urban location. All of this was accomplished with a single design idea of great simplicity: a composition of solids and voids, of huge precast concrete elements and deeply recessed insulating glass fitted beautifully together.

The structure is a hybrid system of precast concrete, poured-in-place concrete and structural steel. The main precast elements are L-shaped columns at the corners supporting 105-ft, 60-ton precast concrete girders. The floor structure consists of steel beams on 10-ft centers spanning from the girders to the 37 ft. 4 in.-square slip-formed concrete core. These beams carry the floor system of metal deck and lightweight concrete slab. The slab is tied compositely to the steel beams by means of studs attached to the top flanges of the beams. Because the structural elements are "dry," very rapid erection was possible.

The concrete building cage is a rigid frame that provides 60 per cent of the lateral stability against wind load; the remaining 40 per cent is provided by the core. The frame was made rigid by using vertical post-tensioning to clamp the corner columns and girders together into a unified structure. Sleeves were cast into the columns and girders in a matched configuration for the vertical post-tensioning rods (see drawing overleaf).

The precast girders were prestressed (via post-tensioning) in the plant to control girder deflection. They were allowed to cure for 23 days prior to post-tensioning.

The girders were hoisted by a pair of 150-ton crawler cranes. Once four of the L-shaped corner columns were in place, a bed of grout was applied to their top horizontal surfaces to receive the girders. After the girders were placed and grout had set, the prestressing rods that extended through sleeves in the girders and columns were post-tensioned to 6,700 psi.

In addition to the vertical sleeves for post-tensioning, the girders and columns have dual-function steel embedments at the ends, on the top horizontal surfaces. Each fitting is comprised of a bearing plate with a short wide-flange stub attached, end-up. After jacks have tensioned the vertical rods, nuts are turned down against the plate to maintain the tension. The WF stubs project up into boxes formed in the bottoms of girders and columns (see drawing). Their purpose is to transfer horizontal shear from girder to column and vice versa.

The corner precast "posts" are essentially filler pieces because they do not participate in the lateral resistance of the frame.

The hvac and lighting systems are designed for a high degree of flexibility

The cooling and heating of the Citizens Bank Center is all-electric. Two 425-ton centrifugal

First step in construction of the tower was slip-forming of the 1-ft thick concrete core. Next was placement of L-shaped corner columns that support the 105-ft precast, post-tensioned girders. Girders were set in position with two crawler cranes. Floor framing is steel beams spanning from the girders to the core. In the corners, steel frames into steel. The floor system is metal deck and a lightweight concrete slab compositely tied to the steel beams.

A multizone air handler with nine zones is provided on each floor. The system is all-electric using electric heaters in ductwork for exterior zone heating.

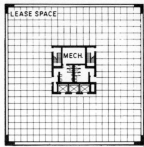

TYPICAL TOWER FLOOR

chillers are located in a central mechanical room at ground level in a secondary location behind retail lease space. Two associated cooling towers are on the roof.

The basic air system uses multi-zone air-handling units of the blow-through type, one unit per floor, each with nine zones for control. Special zoning is provided for corner offices because they have two exposures. Ductwork is of the low-velocity type with acoustical attenuation at the air-handling room to assure a quiet delivery throughout the building.

Heating for perimeter offices is provided by electric duct heaters in the exterior-zone ductwork. There is no heat source in the multizone unit—the normal hot-deck section serves as a by-pass around the cooling units. The temperature controls are set up so that the electric heaters cannot be energized until the dampers are in the full by-pass position, eliminating the possibility of energy-wasting reheat of mechanically-cooled air.

Lighting in the office tower uses 20- by 60-in. recessed troffers of the lay-in type. To provide a nighttime image, the two exterior rows of luminaires are separately circuited with low-voltage (24-v) control. Thus, the building will not be brilliantly illuminated at night, but there will be just enough light so that people will recognize the building as a major structure in the city of Richardson. The control is fully automatic. The lighting can have preselected "time on and time off" control—which can be changed at will.

CITIZENS BANK CENTER, Richardson, Texas. Architects: *OMNIPLAN Architects Harrell + Hamilton*—principal-in-charge: *George F. Harrell;* project manager: *Velpeau Hawes;* designer: *E. G. Hamilton.* Engineers: *Datum Structures Engineering, Inc.* (structural); *Chenault, Brady & Freeman* (mechanical); *Shimek-Roming-Jacobs & Finkles* (civil). Landscape architects: *Myrick, Newman & Dahlber, Inc.* Bank interiors: *Don R. Scott.* Graphics: *OMNIPLAN Design Services.* Market analyst: *Oliver Mattingly.*

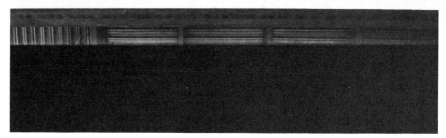

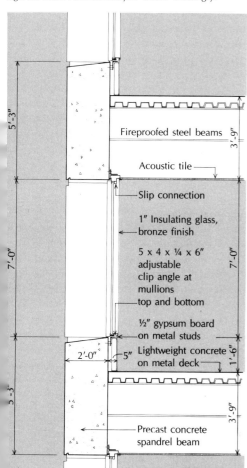

Fireproofed steel beams

Acoustic tile

Slip connection

1" Insulating glass, bronze finish

5 x 4 x ¼ x 6" adjustable clip angle at mullions top and bottom

½" gypsum board on metal studs

5" Lightweight concrete on metal deck

Precast concrete spandrel beam

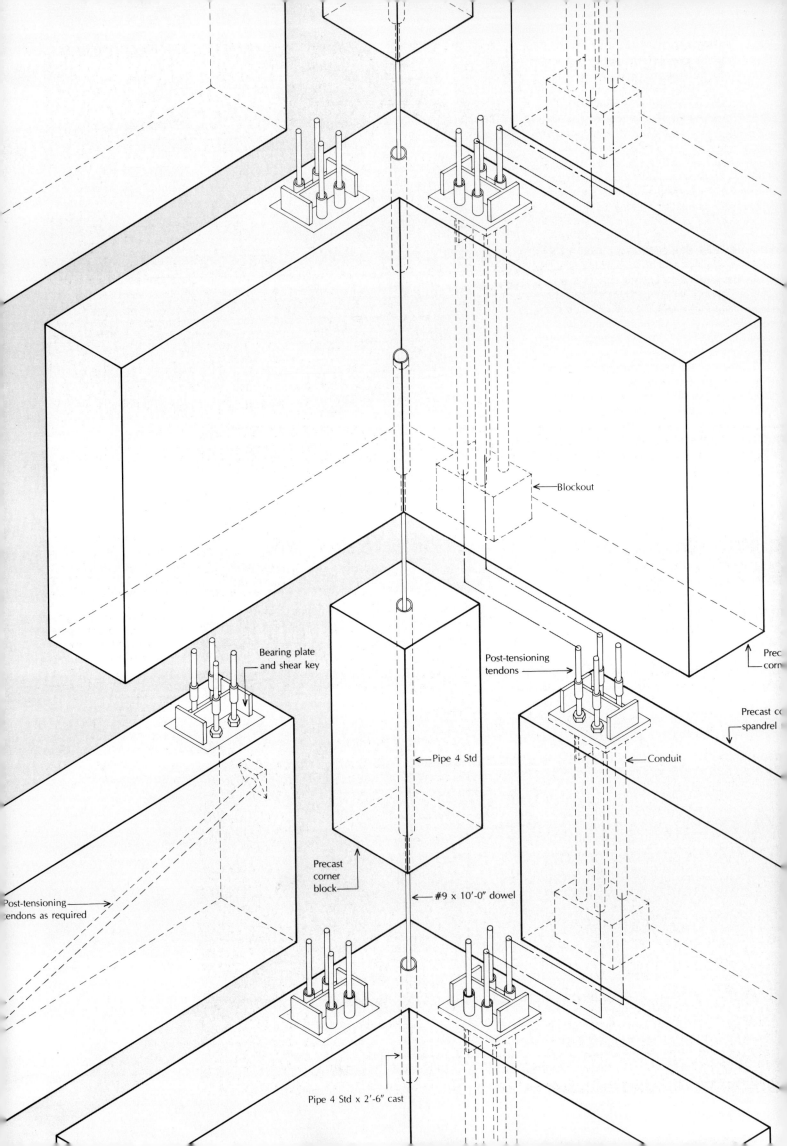

Blockout

Bearing plate
and shear key

Post-tensioning
tendons

Prec
corn

Precast cc
spandrel

Pipe 4 Std

Conduit

Precast
corner
block

Post-tensioning
tendons as required

#9 x 10'-0" dowel

Pipe 4 Std x 2'-6" cast

Citizens Bank Center consists of the bank and an office tower linked by an arcade with retail and restaurant facilities. Entrances to the arcade are located at several points convenient to the major functions and to the parking. The bank's space is situated on two floors with its main lobby and related public functions on the ground level adjacent to the arcade, but secured by a roll-away grille. The ceiling of the banking room (left) is constructed with precast concrete double tees and has skylight wells. A central island houses the teller functions and is connected via a stair to the bookkeeping department directly below.

The width, height and lighting (natural and incandescent) of the arcade are manipulated to create a variety of spaces for pedestrians circulating through the building.

A building respects its landmark neighbors and fits into a plan for revitalizing an entire section of a city

The first major building in Philadelphia's Market Street East Transportation Mall Center—a 20-story glass-walled office building—is an excellent example of design which gives equal attention to the old neighbors (once an important architectural milestone) of the new building and to the integrity of the new building itself, a clearly contemporary design solution.

On one side of 1234 Market Street East, the new building, the Philadelphia Savings Fund Society Building of George Howe and William Lescase, is a 1930 architectural landmark, significant in its time not only as skyscraper design but also as an expression of the best in architecture of that period. On the other side is the much earlier John Wanamaker department store, a handsome building of classic derivation.

Between these two strongly individual and richly atmospheric buildings, 1234 Market East makes a quiet but confident architectural statement of its own time. The glass facade, clear at the base where the public spaces are located and dark for all the floors above, is so restrained and simple that it allows both older buildings to stand in undiminished dignity, respectfully observing the proportions and the lines of its neighbors without in any way diminishing itself.

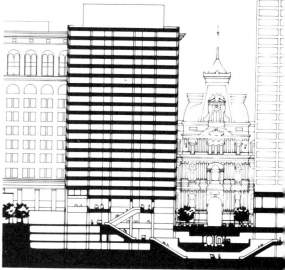

In other ways, not visible from the street, 1234 Market East fits into its neighborhood, not only as it is, but as it is coming to be. The building, because of its location in Philadelphia's big Transportation Mall Center project (to revitalize the entire area), acts as a link in the three-level pedestrian walkway system which leads to a variety of transportation means, and along a skylighted shopping mall. It also connects with the PSFS Building (its original design had anticipated a below-grade concourse) and the Wanamaker store, both below and above the street.

The clear glass base of 1234 Market Street East is not only a break with the two older buildings but a means of disclosing the real function of the street level of this office building: it is public space more than it is a lobby, designed to work integrally with the transportation mall concept, moving people in off-the-street spaces both vertically and horizontally.

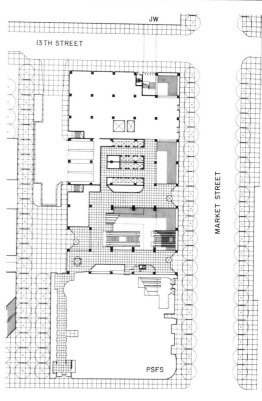

1234 MARKET STREET EAST, Philadelphia, Pennsylvania. Owner/developer: *1234 Associates*. Architects: *Bower & Fradley, George M. Ewing Co.* Engineers: *George M. Ewing Co.* Lighting consultant: *Sylvan R. Shemitz & Associates*. General contractor: *Turner Construction Co.*

5

The distinctive character of this headquarters building for an oil company derives from the skillful handling of simple forms and reflects the client's request that the building be a "strong statement of company image." The same character is carried through to the interior, both in the material used—dark brown brick—and in the handling of forms, producing a working environment of dignity and elegance. The corbelled windows have a functional as well as a visual basis, shielding offices from the strong mountain sun and controlling the panoramic view over Denver and to the front range of the Rocky Mountains. The hilly site, in an industrial park on the outskirts of the city, permits partial screening of the parking area by natural land forms. Outdoor mechanical elements are enclosed in masonry units of material and sculptural form similar to that of the building.

HEADQUARTERS BUILDING, KISSINGER PETROLEUMS LTD., Denver, Colorado. Architects: *RNL, Inc.—John B. Rogers*, partner in charge; *W. Arley Rinehart*, project designer; *Gary Merideth*, interior design. Engineers: *E. Thomas Punshon*, structural; *Kennon B. Stewart*, mechanical; *Behrent Engineering*, electrical. Landscaping: *W. Arley Rinehart*. Contractor: *Hayward Construction Company*.

Ted Tourtelot photos

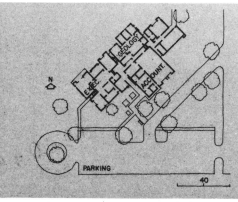

6

The new head office for the Bank of Canada is a multifaceted gem of green-tinted reflective glass trimmed with copper, perched on a rock escarpment across from the Canadian Parliament. By drawing on modern technology and by making use of skilled artisans (Japanese workers pre-patinated the copper trim), the building offers both a foil and a complement for nearby government buildings.

The building comprises two 12-story office towers joined by a Garden Link that also embraces one-third of the existing five-story granite bank, which will house one of the world's outstanding numismatic collections. The Garden Link has been designed for building circulation—a foyer for all three buildings, plus bridges connecting the towers—and for public amenity (for one thing, a respite from Ottawa's cold winter weather).

The skylighted area has two layers of glass between which conditioned air is circulated to prevent condensation and to melt snow in winter. Perforated copper-trimmed spandrels supply a curtain of air to the glass walls of the Garden Link. The inner portions of the engaged columns serve as vertical plenums for the spandrels. The building is sheathed with reflective double-glazing.

Because Ottawa is in Seismic Risk Zone 2 (VII on Richter scale) the Garden Link structure—essentially a stiff diaphragm on "sticks" —has its roof structure pinned to one of the office towers and has a sliding joint at the other, so it can move independently of the stiff concrete office frames.

Inside the towers, a structure of concrete "trees" on a 30-ft module incorporates the lighting, mechanical and electrical systems. The structure embodies a great number of functional and planning advantages. It provides "natural" channels for routing services, and "umbrellas" to reflect indirect light. It reduces the number of columns to a minimum, and eliminates them entirely around the windows. It provides solid concrete members into which partitions can frame. And it gives a sense of territory to small groups in the open-office scheme.

BANK OF CANADA, Ottawa. Architects: *Marani, Rounthwaite & Dick* and *Arthur Erickson,* associated architects—*Ronald Dick* (administrative partner-in-charge), *Arthur Erickson* (design partner-in-charge), *James Strasman* (project design architect). Engineers: *C.D. Carruthers & Wallace* (structural); *ARDEC Consulting Engineers* and *Brais, Frigon* (mechanical/electrical). Consultants: *William M. C. Lam* (lighting); *Emil van der Meullen* (landscape architect).

Two 12-story office towers are joined by a climate-controlled Garden Link that serves as a foyer, a bridge between the towers and as a public space.

Robert E. Fischer photos

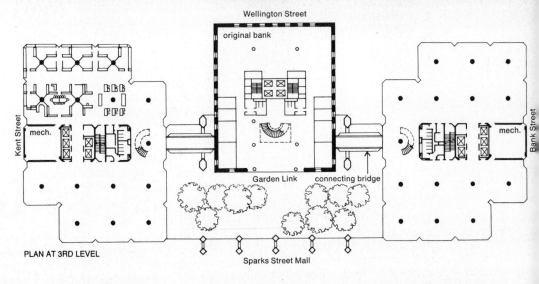

Wellington Street

original bank

Kent Street

Bank Street

mech.

mech.

Garden Link   connecting bridge

PLAN AT 3RD LEVEL

Sparks Street Mall

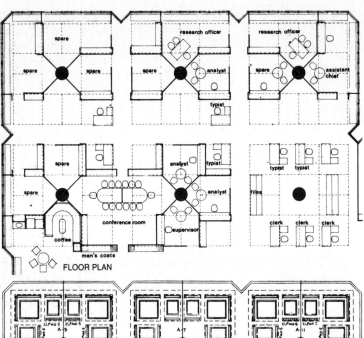

FLOOR PLAN

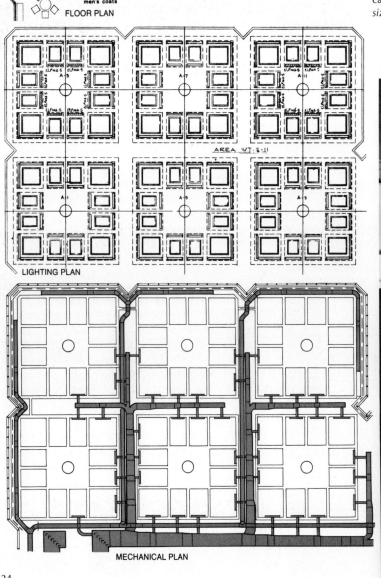

AREA WT-3-11

LIGHTING PLAN

MECHANICAL PLAN

The structural system is a series of independent structural trees, 30 ft on center. Each tree has a 3-ft-dia. column supporting a 25-ft capital composed of 3-ft-deep ribs cantilevering from a drop head in the center.

This system creates a 5-ft-wide space around each tree, providing service space for air ducts, wiring and lighting ballasts. The underside of the channel has a suspended ceiling for access. The "umbrella" portion of the trees was made 3 ft deep to accommodate services, and not for structural reasons—though this depth did save reinforcing steel. Similarly, the rib spacing was chosen not for structural reasons but to provide convenient locations for partitions and properly sized coffers for lighting.

Each cell created by the ceiling had to provide air supply and return (via slotted boxes attached to the lighting units), lighting (via direct/indirect luminaires), plug-in electrical distribution (via an electrified track around the "lid" of each coffer which allows use of accent lighting and the installation of power poles, if required), and sound absorption (via acoustical panels in the coffers). Lighting level is 90-120 footcandles (initial); office furniture is light oak, and carpet is tan/beige.

In a practice being used increasingly in Canada (for flexibility and smoke control), there are independent "package" mechanical rooms for each floor of the office towers. The low-pressure fans use only about one-half as much energy as high-pressure fans with centralized mechanical rooms.

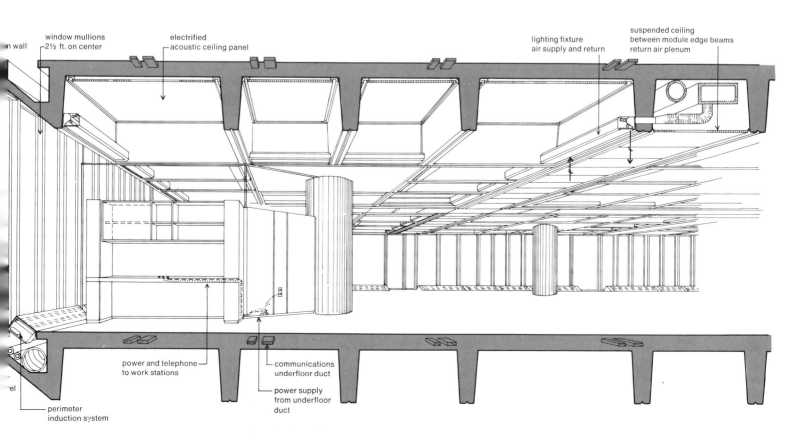

window mullions 2½ ft. on center

electrified acoustic ceiling panel

lighting fixture air supply and return

suspended ceiling between module edge beams return air plenum

power and telephone to work stations

communications underfloor duct

power supply from underfloor duct

perimeter induction system

7

It is hard to beat Butler Square, until recently a burly red brick pile of a warehouse on the edge of Minneapolis' resurgent downtown, as a case-example of the new appreciation of reuse or, supplying a touchstone of architecture's transition to the new attitudes. The reason is that this massive encrustation of thick walls, deeply recessed windows, arched entrances, corbeled cornices, and rampart-like towers is a lesson-laden example of what that articulate Englishman, Alex Gordon, said should be the primary premises of design strategy in coming years—"long life, loose fit, low energy." These are words that deserve to ring sonorously through the ages as have, say, "firmness, commodity, and delight." Design strategy can be heavy stuff, of course, especially when it comes up against, as it inevitably must, something even heavier— spending strategy. This is precisely what Gordon's thinking is directed at in contrast to most of the conceptual catch-phrases that have come and gone, over the last three-quarters of a century, in association with those "schools of thought" making up what has been called (get ready) The Modern Movement. It can be said that the Butler *really* did it because, for a strikingly low cost, this Teddy Roosevelt period-piece, put up in 1906, has been turned into a working combine of commercial, business, and public spaces. Not only that, it looks as though the place is, on the heels of a harrowing rent-up rate resulting from the sluggish economy, going to turn a profit, which also means, as such things go, that this wintry city of 430,000 skate-toting sports is going to have some tax revenue drifting in that it would not have had otherwise. Not everything has been jim-dandy about this job, as if everything about any job *ever* is. What is material here, besides an ardent adaptation of brick and timber, is the fact that it is still damned difficult to convince potential investors of the economic feasibility of taking a 70-year-old shard—even one singled out for national landmark status, as the Butler has been—and turning it into something other than it was originally. Oh, sure. It makes one feel mighty good to be able to say, "Ah ha. Told you so. And for just $20 per square foot." But the real story behind this building—or, so it would appear, inside—is what kind of cajoling and convincing it took to get to the point where there were dollars to pay for the proof. This connection between economics and esthetics has always existed—one of the most enduring, encompassing tendencies of culture. Physical durability, functional lee-way, budgetary thrift—the Butler makes the connection clear. Given the constraints of a believable bottom-line, and the necessity of stretching available resources, here is a bellwether ringing with beauty.

There is a certain legibility in the ordinary warehouses that are found on the back blocks of our cities. Looking at them, it is possible to make out what such a city has been about, or even plans to be. For these are structures where shirt-sleeved breadwinners helped write urban history in the course of doing, as the old saw says, an honest day's work for an honest day's pay. These plain, purposeful chips off the old American block are, even when idle, vivid with imagery and, especially when idle, with immediacy as well. A structure in place is a compaction of space, materials, and bound-up energy—all at the ready for resuscitation and renewed community service. There are few things as legible in these troubled times because society has squandered so many of its resources in its gluttonous pursuit of material gain. In feeding the forces of conservation, helping redefine and redirect the impetus for change, an honest day's work for an honest day's pay becomes a new saw for financing, designing, and operating buildings.

This is why the Butler Brothers Building in Minneapolis, now renamed Butler Square, is such a benchmark, not only one in terms of adapting older structures for new uses but, far more importantly, in terms of basic values that are applicable to spanking new structures.

The Butler, idle for 10 years, is back in business as an eye-catching collage of commercial, retail, and business activity that ranges up and around a skylit nine-story atrium. Here are office suites which, like lairs on the ledges of a chasm wall, look out upon one of the most animated but articulate public spaces to be created anywhere in recent years. Lively shops, cozy corners to sip or sup in, landscaped promenades to stroll along, spots just to sit—it's all here and, as one secretary put it recently, "I find that I'm in no particular hurry to leave at night." Such ebullience puts one in mind of something which that old architecture buff, Charles Laughton, once did upon entering a new structure by one of his favorite designers. Rotund and affable, he spread out his arms as if to hug the space and shouted, "Why can't *I* work here?" A lot of people around town have been having a similar reaction to the explosion of life and light within the recently sandblasted austerity of the Butler's thick and slightly mysterious exterior walls, which resemble some sort of Tuscan fortress. Inside, these walls encase a not-slightly sensational experience, a bounteous and beautiful

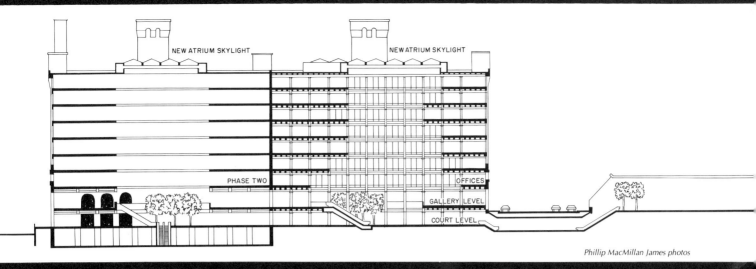

NEW ATRIUM SKYLIGHT　　　　NEW ATRIUM SKYLIGHT

PHASE TWO　　　　　　　　　　OFFICES

GALLERY LEVEL

COURT LEVEL

Phillip MacMillan James photos

space bounded by the expressive edge of the building's fir-timber construction.

This phase of the project takes up half of the building's 500,000 square feet which, need it be said, is a lot of room. Work is shortly to begin on the second half, which is being adapted as a 300-room hotel called Butler House—something that is badly needed in business-busy Minneapolis. None other than Investors Diversified Services (IDS) will manage it and, so the company reports, the three hotels it already owns are presently turning away the equivalent of 60 per cent of occupancy. No two ways about it, the Butler is an example of the past which is right on time and, considering this town's adventuresome plans for reweaving its fabric, it is even in the right place—something that can not be said for many proposed renovations, many of which never get anywhere precisely because the buildings at issue are located in areas beyond salvage or, if not, in areas where most people wouldn't dream of setting foot. The Butler's surrounds, while a little seedy with parking lots, gas stations, bars, and assorted porn-on-the-cob Americana, are not only salvageable but, because of all those "eyes of the Street," as Jane Jacobs used to say, are even safe.

The Butler counterpoints some of the nation's finest contemporary architecture. Most alluring, perhaps, is the IDS Center, but a few blocks away, designed by Philip Johnson. Its energetic masses shimmer around an expansive covered court in much the same uplifting mix of people and purpose that characterizes Butler Square. Taking the outside inside, one of The Modern Movement's early tenets, seems to be reviving here in Minneapolis with an especially urbane *elan*. Another variation of the idea is at John Carl Warnecke's Hennepin County building, a two-tower extravaganza connected by a skyscraping atrium that is, in turn, interlaced with varied levels, bridges, and bright landscaping.

The Butler was originally done by architect Harry W. Jones and built by T. B. Walker, who founded the Walker Arts Center. The new handiwork is by fine local talent, the firm of Miller, Hanson, Westerbeck, Bell in collaboration with Arvid Elness, the project architect in his days with MHWB who is serving as project manager on the second phase of work.

Here are some of the reasons this particular architectural team gets high marks. First of all, they didn't try to put on the dog and foist

The sand-blasted sobriety of Butler Square's thick exterior walls is embellished with planting and banners (top), concealing the spacious, nine-story atrium inside (center and opposite page) around which rise promenades, commercial areas, and office suites. The tactile quality of the building is immediately clear (bottom) at the entrance where the brick-and-timber grammar of the original work grabs hold of the senses before releasing them inside.

some notion of contemporary form upon an existing one. In what might be called the ultimate in originality, they deferred to that of the old building and kept their own quiet.

The Butler's interior stems from a succinct structural system. The heavy fir timbers taken from Walker's own tree farm and lumber mill way out in tiny Aitken, Minnesota, were put together on a module measuring about 16 by 14 feet. The columns, which receive the beams with cast-iron brackets, gradually diminish in size from 22 inches square on the ground floor to a spindly eight inches near the top. The atrium was created by disassembling this timber system toward the center of the building, and the removed material was then recycled to provide consistent details and finishes in the occupied areas.

The atrium is economic in nature, not just esthetic—as dramatic a visual event as it is. Without a substantial amount of its floor space given over to this, the 250,000 square feet that this phase takes up of the over-all building would have yielded floors of too vast a size to be well enough lighted or to be broken up in the more intimate configurations thought to be marketable in the "luxury" field.

This result, as architect Elness explains, "retains a certain integrity. No attempt was made to conceal elements of the existing structure." On the exterior, minimal change took place and, in fact, minimal change is all that was possible. "The only visible alteration," he says, "is the lowering of the window spandrel to accommodate pedestrian access at grade level, and that of floor-to-ceiling glass in the office areas." These modifications are limited to the original lines of the building so as not to detract from its somber simplicity.

Inside, these lines, expressing the elegant egg-crate effect of the structure, are like hyped up vectors—racing one's sight and senses this way and that. The first two levels contain the commercial and retail activity around the tiled floor of the skylit atrium which, at this point, is landscaped plentifully and colorfully. The upper seven levels contain the offices—a wide variety of them, in fact. The module of the building, horizontally and vertically, proved to be marvelously flexible, and every floor, reflecting a lively mix of tenants, has turned out differently. While there may be a few tenants occupying large floor areas, the space concept was conceived along the lines of dividing each floor into quadrants, with the offices in each one ranging from 114 to 400 square feet. Yet

within each quadrant is still more flexibility, because, if more than one tenant is involved, the quadrant is accordingly adapted so that reception, secretarial, storage, and reference functions can be shared.

A feeling of cohesion between areas is supplied by the structural frame—one of material bearing and visual orientation—but, within this discipline, the almost communal vigor of the place can be readily grasped as the glassed-in offices overlooking the atrium reveal themselves through the hand-me-down curtain-wall of timbers.

It is here that the imagery of ordinary utilitarian buildings like this is most compelling, and the immediacy of their use to accommodating present-day needs so clear. Very little tinkering was needed to achieve the effect and, where tinkering did occur, it is not noticeable. For example, electrical, mechanical, and air-conditioning equipment is slid under a slightly raised floor surface so that the overhead beams and ceiling timbers could be retained and thus texture the place with tangible warmth. Even with such typical paraphernalia as overhead sprinklers, boxed lighting fixtures and, throughout, partitions of good old gypsum board, these offices are anything but the dumb fluorescent-lit deserts that routinely parch the environment of deep-down appeal—"efficiency"—while sending us working stiffs screaming for the nearest saloon at five.

The most important dimension, however, was measured by the developer of Butler Square—Charles B. Coyer of Washington, D.C.—who has always had a thing for old buildings and, having a thing for making them work financially, dramatized the profit potential of recycling them a few years ago with his much-acclaimed Canal Square in historic Georgetown.

Successful in having secured financing so far—the General Electric Pension Trust should be given an AIA medal for having taken the step to back the Butler Square phase—Coyer, still trying to mobilize money for Phase Two, is hardly sanguine in discussing the recurrent obstacles.

"With dollars so tight," he comments, "and with investors justifiably concerned about slow rent-ups, there was probably not a worse time to try to find money for this. We eventually reached a break even point with 75 per cent rented, but for a while there, things were pretty much touch and go. It is not that there were no interested parties but, a year

The original design features of Butler Square have been set off rather than shown up by the recent conversion such as (top) the retention of the early entrances and window openings enhanced by simple sheets of glass and unobtrusive fixtures, the powerful character of the interior atrium made possible by the disassembly of part of the timber frame, and the warm, sensate quality of the varied offices (bottom) that derives from having retained the natural materials throughout.

ago, there were a lot of clouds in the future of a lot of firms, and it was naturally difficult for them to make a move. Now, with things looking a little brighter, we've found an encouraging number who stayed bullish on the place and are coming back to reconsider.

"But the single greatest challenge in our field today is convincing the financial community, even in the best of times, that just because a building is 70 years old doesn't mean that it's not a good investment. The fact is that, in the long term, it can be one of the best but, the trouble is, investors still tend to figure in a dollar-figure for what it thought of as depreciation. And the reason they still do is that there is a feeling that something old is automatically of less monetary value; in other words, they decide on the basis of the existing shell instead of on the basis of what value might accrue as a result of what is done with, or within, that shell. So what happens is this. Say you figure that you need $6 million. The investor is liable to offer you in the neighborhood of $5 million or, in tough times, even less. Once you add up all the finance charges and other fees, it is not unusual for the actual amount of money put in by investors to amount to only 25 per cent of the over-all cost of accomplishing the job, and by accomplishing the job I mean all the costs of getting to the point where, with adequate income from rents, you can turn a profit."

Butler Square is the complete conversion—evidence that a strategically sited building, located in an area that has been declared ripe for renewal otherwise, can be turned to the service of commonly recognized commercial and business needs.

But more than this, it is a reminder, in fundamental design terms, that the resources of the past and the requirements of the present day not only hinge upon each other in these belt-tight times. They can enhance each other. While it is recognized today that the profession of architecture is in a state of retrenchment, it is also in a state of reflection. At Butler Square there are elements of both, and a good look at architecture's future—as it really was.

BUTLER SQUARE, Minneapolis, Minnesota. Owner *Development Associates, Washington, D.C.* Architects: *Miller, Hanson, Westerbeck, Bell (in collaboration with Arvid Elness, project architect).* Engineers: *Frank Horner (structural); TAC Engineering (electrical and plumbing); Temperature Engineering Corp. (heating and ventilation systems).* Contractor *Knutson Co.*

Nick Wheeler photos

8

At the AIA Convention in San Francisco in May 1973, Johns-Manville announced that The Architects Collaborative was the winner of a competition among nine selected firms for the design of its new headquarters on a ranch near the outskirts of Denver. Not long afterward, construction got underway — almost before the TAC team had recovered from their victory — and the results are spectacular. What is most remarkable is the degree to which the reality of the building is faithful to the dream of the winning design. This took courage on the part of Johns-Manville; tenacity from TAC; flexibility from Turner Construction Company, the construction managers; and brilliance from William LeMessurier, the structural engineer, for his innovative work in "plastic design" of the long span structure with a minimum of steel. The extraordinary strength and beauty of the building in its magnificent setting is shown in the photos beginning overleaf. The successful struggle among contending forces to create this work of architecture is described on the following pages.

The building is sited as splendidly as a Greek temple. It occupies the land sparingly, yet powerfully, as it reflects the changes, by hour and season, of the desert sky. If great landscapes must be built upon, it is best to touch them lightly. For J-M, automobile circulation was a primary design factor, and 300 cars can be parked on the roof and on the parabolic tiers carved into the uphill slope. From many vantage points, however, the building appears to be visited and served in secret, the landscape unmarred by the paraphernalia of the automobile. The building itself, however, is no secret. Unlike Taliesin West, for an example, which is built of desert materials, the J-M building is an avowedly machine-made object.

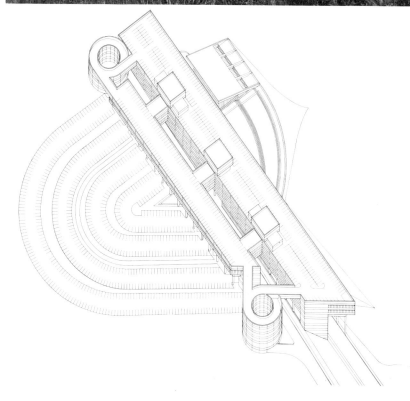

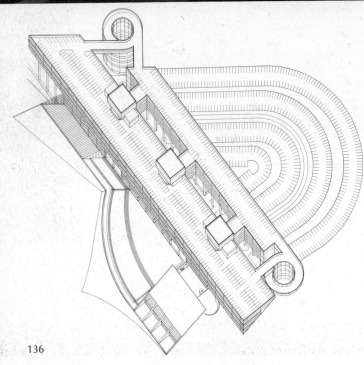

The axonometric shows two projecting wedge-shaped forms the smaller of which is a greenhouse connected to the stately arcs of the pool by a terrace, and the larger a cafeteria. As can be seen in the photographs (middle left and opposite page), the greenhouse has not been built—unfortunately, since the pool and terrace need to be precisely contained by a second form and the cafeteria needs to be balanced visually by another projecting element. This dining facility has a friendly scale which partially counteracts the awesome horizontal stretch of the building, but the other scale-reducing shape is needed. A greenhouse would help the transition from indoors to outdoors.

The coming together of the Johns-Manville Corporation and The Architects Collaborative in the persons of W.R. Goodwin, J-M's former president, and Joseph D. Hoskins, until recently a principal at TAC, had everything to do with the fact that this corporate headquarters building is so spectacular. Although both men have moved on, Goodwin to found another company and Hoskins to start his own architectural practice, they have left behind them a building that reflects great credit upon J-M and TAC.

Goodwin was president of Johns-Manville during the period in which the company bought a 10,000-acre ranch, 22 miles from downtown Denver to become the site of its new headquarters; moved its personnel from New York City to temporary offices in Denver to await the construction of its proposed building; and held a limited design competition to find an architect for this facility. The building was substantially completed at the time Goodwin resigned.

From the beginning, Joseph Hoskins was TAC's man in charge of winning the competition against stiff competition—Welton Becket and Associates, Caudill Rowlett Scott, Inc., Vincent G. Kling & Partners, Neuhaus and Taylor, I.M. Pei & Partners, William L. Pereira Associates, RTKL, Inc. and Sert, Jackson and Associates, Inc. As principal-in-charge for TAC he saw the building through to completion, defending its design integrity against the many challenges that inevitably arose during the construction process. Goodwin unfailingly backed up Hoskins throughout this period.

TAC won the competition for the masterful way Hoskins and his team placed the building on its site, using the foothills as a backdrop and building up against them, for the bold manner in which the architects took advantage of the vista toward Denver across an undefiled valley, for their elegant and minimal design of the roadway approach with its dramatic arrival under the building, and for their unobtrusive insertion of parking space on the roof and in tiers carved into the natural bowls at the rear of the building. The jury, chaired by architect Harry Weese and including Goodwin, architects Theodore C. Bernardi and Robert Geedes, and Hubertus J. Mittmann—regional landscape architect for the United States Forest Service, Rocky Mountain region in Denver—commended TAC's de-

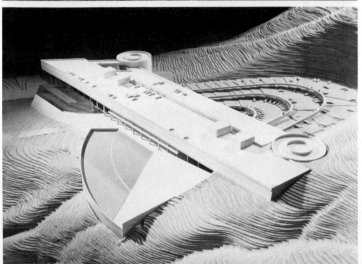

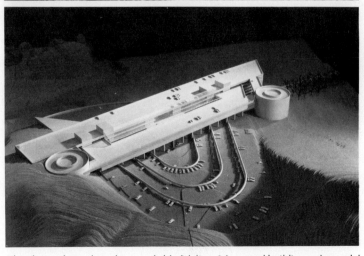

The photos above show the remarkable fidelity of the actual building to the model of the winning design.

sign for combining all the elements—parking terraces, helix ramps, reflecting pools, greenhouse (unfortunately not built) and open ground—into a sculptural composition of great interest and variety which had the potential of forming a very distinctive image from the air. The latter was an important consideration. Johns-Manville executives fly in and out in the company helicopter and the building can be seen at high altitude from the transcontinental flight path.

Mastering the site

Anyone who has flown out of Denver toward the Rockies in a small low-flying aircraft has seen a long ridge rising abruptly from the plain like a great wall of rock stretching to infinity. This ridge, called the "hogbacks," announces the beginning of the Rockies. Just beyond the hogbacks is a valley sloping westward to the foothills. The hogbacks start near Boulder and come to an end just south of the Johns-Manville ranch. They form a vista from the site which is unique. From the foothills of the mountains, which are included on the J-M property, one can look across the valley and through the hogbacks to the city of Denver, 22 miles away.

For TAC the design process began with a helicopter tour of the site. Said Hoskins: "I was looking for a location for the building that would make the most of what was there. The Rockies are great as seen from Denver, or when you are up in them, but the foothills as seen from the front range are not that spectacular. The most beautiful portion of the site is the valley itself as bounded by the hogbacks. I determined that we shouldn't build in the valley, but up on the edge of the mountains to encompass the view across it. The landscape architects on our team told me the site I wanted was unbuildable because the slopes were too steep, but we went ahead anyway, confident we could solve the site engineering problems as they arose.'

The TAC design team next made a model at the scale of 2 feet to 100 miles. The building was tiny at that scale, but downtown Denver was on the model and so were the hogbacks and foothills. TAC wanted the building to be tied to Denver by a vista—an idea as old as architecture. The architects made further studies to determine the best wind and sun orientations and went on to consider the problems of access and parking.

The building site the TAC team selected was not ideal fo

parking because it had very little flat land. J-M did not want to build a parking garage and had asked the competitors to come up with an imaginative outdoor parking solution. Hoskins wanted to make the parking an intrinsic part of the design of the building. Since he intended to make the structure long and low, providing the square footage called for by the program in as few floors as possible and thus providing the maximum square footage per floor, he knew that he could put many of the required parking spaces on the wide and long roof which would result. Further parking, the team reasoned, could be carved into one or more of the bowl-shaped natural forms on the building site. They envisioned that this carved space in the back, essentially closed, would be an effective contrast to the vastness of the space and view on the other side of the building. Early in the design, when the building was more linear, two bowls were carved into parking tiers, but as the building became less long and more wide, one bowl was settled upon.

Although the parked cars and access roads are scarcely visible from many viewpoints within the building and on the site, the movement and accommodation of the automobile shaped the building as much as did considerations of orientation and vista. The J-M employee driving to work is within the design as soon as the building appears on the horizon. He enters the structure by car between the two wings, turns into the parking lot or drives up one of the helix ramps to the roof. This automotive circulation system was kept extremely simple in order to be legible at driving speed, and it is completely separated from pedestrian pathways. It was, however, not so simple to devise.

According to Hoskins: "Four days before our submission was due we totally changed the design. We went five days without sleep. We barely got it on the plane. We barely got it there. We changed the design because the automobile circulation was unclear, the metaphorical recalls were not clear, and the entrance was not cleanly worked out. All the relationships were wrong—water, cafeteria, everything. We changed the approach, the circulation, the ramps and everything they affected. The metaphorical quality we sought finally emerged—the metaphor of the building as a bridge between morning and evening in which the day's work takes

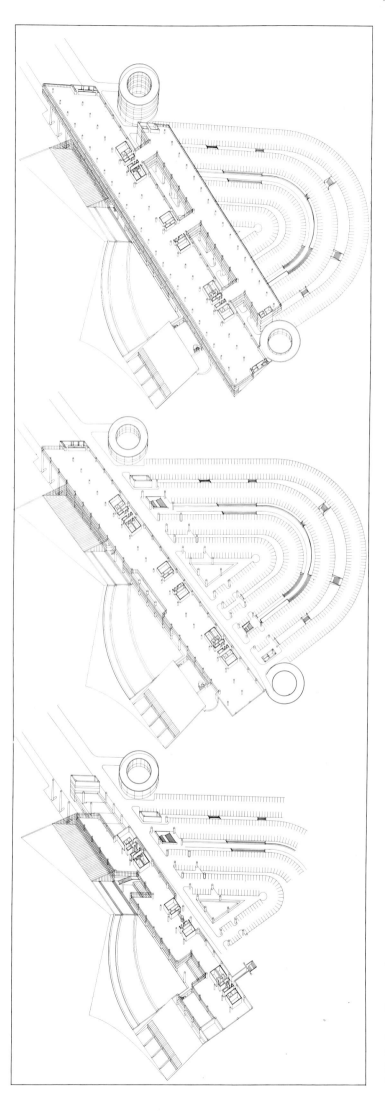

place. Coming to work one drives to the bridge, lives in the bridge and drives away from it toward home. When we got it right we had to rebuild the model. It was an incredible charette. The model-making firm had thrown in the towel so John Sheehy and I started to put it together and the rest of the team assembled it at the last minute in Denver. Since I think our earlier design would have won as well, but since construction of our winning design began almost immediately, with no time for further significant change, I'm glad we fixed it when we did."

Taking a chance
Anyone comparing TAC's design with the submissions of the eight other firms would note the elegant clarity of TAC's building, the simplicity of its shapes, the strength of its image, and contrast it favorably with the others, all of which were extraordinarily complicated and seemingly confused by comparison. Since TAC'S competitors are all architects of stature, the question is—what happened? The answer is that the TAC team boldly deviated from the program because it could not have been successfully solved as written. The others did not. TAC won hands down.

The program established a poorly conceived ratio between linear feet of building perimeter and net square foot floor area which forced the other architects into surrounding relatively small portions of space with perimeter wall. This led to meandering plans with lots of ins and outs, or to multi-story pavilions strung together like beads on a necklace. Only a high-rise building could have successfully accommodated this ratio, but this was not considered a valid alternative by any of the competitors.

Hoskins had recently worked on another TAC project, the Shawmut Bank, which had demanded that the architects provide large floors. The bankers believed that large floor areas facilitate communication and that good communication is one of the secrets of successful business. Hoskins thought that large floors would be advantageous to Johns-Manville. Therefore he discounted the importance of the perimeter module as given but worked with the established floor areas reducing the linear feet of perimeter wall. This gave him the opportunity to develop a simpler building form and to take brilliant advantage of the opportunities offered by the site.

The other buildings as designed were too sprawling and amorphous to perch in the foothills overlooking the valley. Each one had to be located somewhere on the valley floor—the wrong place as TAC's design makes clear.

Ideally, of course, office landscaping should have been used in TAC's building so that more employees would have a view from their work spaces. The J-M management preferred offices with floor-to-ceiling partitions, however, so the space was planned to allow all the employees to enjoy the view at various communal gathering points such as terraces and the cafeteria. This works very well.

TAC's gamble with the program paid off handsomely, but it is to the jury's credit that on the strength of Hoskin's design, they also decided to discount the perimeter ratio and declare TAC the winner.

The construction manager's role
Although the final completion of the building was held up because of delays in the fabrication of the aluminum skin, the Johns-Manville employees began moving in on schedule, as work continued around them. Costs were kept within a total of $66 million. The Turner Construction Company considers this performance an excellent example of the value of construction expertise under conditions far from the ordinary. They point out that the construction site was over a mile from the nearest road and three miles from a major highway, making accessibility difficult. The siting of the building on the sloped side of the Rocky Mountain foothills, although wonderful, presented special problems. In the beginning there were no water or other utilities on the site, and the sheer size of the project (750,000 gross square feet), made it among the biggest ever constructed in Colorado. The 1070-foot-long building, if stood on end, would be the tallest west of the Mississippi River.

The building was dedicated on July 4, 1976, two years and nine months after construction was begun in October 1973. Work began promptly, approximately five months after the winning competitor was announced on May 7, 1973 at the AIA Convention in San Francisco. The TAC team had barely ceased celebrating when Turner was selected by Johns-Manville and TAC to be construction manager. According to Douglas Meyer, general superintendent

of Turner's Denver office: "The first thing we did was prepare cost estimates on TAC's schematic designs."

Despite the lack of detailed information, Turner was able to make early cost estimates to determine the approximate quantities of major items, such as excavation, structural steel, curtain wall, concrete and pouring material for the one-and-a-half-mile road that had to be built to reach the site. This schematic design phase was concluded in late September 1973, only four months after Turner joined the building team.

Immediately following came the design development stage which continued through early 1974, while excavation had begun. During this period Turner worked with TAC and Johns-Manville on the consideration of a number of alternative building systems. Budget figures were developed for each of the contract packages and agreed upon with TAC and Johns-Manville to become the final budget.

Following agreement on the budget estimate, Turner developed a comprehensive project schedule using a computerized "Project Scheduling System" developed a comprehensive project schedule using a computerized "Project Scheduling System" developed by the firm a few years before. "The system allows us to establish the over-all sequence of events with start and finish dates for each of the trades, lead times and milestone dates for all design and construction activities," Douglas Meyer explains.

Throughout the design phases of the project, a major function of Turner was to provide accurate cost estimates of the major alternate methods and systems being considered by the architect, as well as their availability and any labor situation which might affect the performance of any particular aspect of the work.

Central to Turner's success as construction manager at J-M was its use of the fast-track schedule, which helped keep costs as low as possible in a period of rapid price escalation, as well as keeping the project moving on time by pre-purchasing of materials. As an example, Joseph Consigli, general manager, real estate for J-M, cites the early purchase of structural steel well before completion of the final skin design as saving more than six months of price inflation estimated at between $250,000 and $500,000. Other prepur-

chased materials were stored at the site, and subcontractors and suppliers were reimbursed for advance deliveries of materials and equipment.

In all, Meyer estimates that total savings to Johns-Manville through the use of the fast-track method total over $2 million on steel and other materials and systems.

It was after consideration of all these factors that Turner prepared final estimates that were then accepted and became a guaranteed maximum price for the duration of the project. It was procedures such as these and the early and continuing interaction among TAC, Turner and J-M that produced such impressive results in terms of schedule and budgets.

Also crucial to the success of the project, Meyer emphasizes, was the acceptance of responsibility and prompt decision making where and when necessary by J-M's Joseph Consigli. Says Meyer: "Phased construction under a construction management process requires decisiveness on the part of the owner and a willingness by the owner's representative to serve as the key figure for moderating between all parties. Joe Consigli's prompt and authoritative action throughout the project was a key to its success."

Prefabricating the skin
The J-M building has one of the most beautiful aluminum curtain walls ever seen. It is illuminated by a wide open desert sky, of course, and changes magnificently with the light, so much of the credit for its splendor must go to nature. But it doesn't "tin can," its color is even, its joints are precise. The skilled hand of man must be praised also as it labored in the drafting rooms of TAC and the fabricator. What makes this skin so wonderfully smooth and flat?

In the system developed by TAC and the fabricator's engineers, the panel skin is not welded to the stiffeners. Instead the panel is essentially "hung" on the stiffeners and allowed to ride "free" or "float." The stiffeners are anchored to the building as before, and provide the necessary bracing to meet performance specifications. As temperatures change, the panel skin changes dimension but—since it is not confined by welds—it does not distort. Color uniformity of the panels was checked by means of electronic color quality control equipment in the fabrication plant.

Planning the interiors
The interior design and planning of all the spaces within the J-M building, including the cafeteria, with its long views, is the work of The Space Design Group. That firm helped write the competition program that spelled out Johns-Manville's needs based upon their working knowledge of the company, its collective personnel needs, its physical requirements, and its corporate personality.

As pointed out earlier, the ultimate shape of the building did not reflect the wall-perimeter specifications called for by The Space Design Group in their program—but the shape provided the firm with interesting design opportunities—and also posed certain interior design problems.

One such problem was the treatment of the long passageways, which were an intrinsic part of the TAC design. Usually attempts are made by interior designers to obscure the length and regularity of such corridors. In the J-M complex, however, The Space Design Group saw these long arteries (several of them more than 1,000 feet in length) as an opportunity for drama. The interior designers used no artificial light in these corridors, but rather illuminated them with the light filtering through the glass that forms the upper level of the office partitions, and by the much greater quantities of light pouring in at the intervals where there are no partitions. These intervals occur at the secretarial areas every one of which is opened to the exterior of the building.

To dramatize these major arteries further, the ceilings have been lowered and the partitions have a reflective laminate surface.

JOHNS-MANVILLE WORLD HEAD-QUARTERS, Jefferson County, Colorado. Owner: Johns-Manville Sale Corporation. Architects: The Architects Collaborative — principal-in-charge: Joseph D. Hoskins; project architect for design: John P. Sheehy, Michael Gebhart; project architects for documents: Vernon Herzeelle, Eugene Hayes; team: Valdis Smits, Spence Tart, Dushan Stankovich, Sam Farr, Alexis Morgan, Michael Miller; Robert DeWolfe and David Mittelstadt (landscape); Walter Rosenfeld (specifications); Harish Patel (graphics). Associate architect: Carl F. Groos, J Consultants: LeMessurier Associates SCI (structural); Golder, Gass Associates, Inc. (foundations); Cosentini Associates (mechanical, electrical, acoustical and lighting); The Space Design Group (interiors). Construction manager: Turner Construction Co.

9

To provide a new organization and visual focus to the mammoth
twenty-five year old Westinghouse Medium-Speed Elevator assembly plant,
architects Bohlin and Powell have designed an administration
building through which the plant workers pass daily. Built with
economic industrial materials—like a central skylit "street"—and
containing its important features where they count, the office building
raises the morale of office and the adjacent factory's workers
alike.

Westinghouse, Medium-speed Elevator Division

Long a leader in commitment to good design, Westinghouse began operations of this plant in Randolph Township, New Jersey, in 1952. The original 420,000-square-foot manufacturing building was designed by Skidmore, Owings & Merrill. When there was a need for expansion of offices and research, the corporation turned to architects Bohlin and Powell, who first examined the idea of placing the new spaces (32,000 square feet were required in the first stage) on top of the plant in a location that was central to operations and that avoided the usual "tacked-on" appearance of plant office space. But costs and circulation were impossible in the integrated scheme, and the architects turned to examine how an addition might become a positive asset to the rural site of 150 acres, and an organizing element for the whole plant.

Accordingly, a new focus was created by directing the access road toward the new building and reinforcing the new axis with rows of trees, which also shielded the initial view of the older production facility. The focus will, in the future, be further reinforced with a test tower next to the entrance, which is shared by visitors, and plant and office workers alike; and it is reinforced by the inviting glass roof over the spaces within.

In creating the form of the addition, Bohlin and Powell did not try to create a unique piece of architecture wherein all of the parts were equally as important. The building has an economical steel frame, and is simple and straightforward—with only selected parts accentuated by special treatment—the glazed corridor, one curve in the corridor wall, and the rounded fascia above the entrance that reflects light from any direction and spells "entrance." The sheathing is an extension of the original plant's polished, mill-finished aluminum skin. Such economy of means is not only appropriate but helped to bring the building within low, allowable construction cost—and helped the architects win a Pennsylvania AIA award.

MEDIUM-SPEED ELEVATOR DIVISION, Randolph Township, New Jersey. Owner: *Westinghouse Electric Corporation.* Architects: *Bohlin and Powell*—partner-in-charge: *Peter Bohlin;* project architect: *Donald Maxwell.* Engineers: *Vincent Szykman, Inc.* (structural); *Paul H. Yeomans, Inc.* (mechanical/electrical). General contractor: *Goltra Construction.*

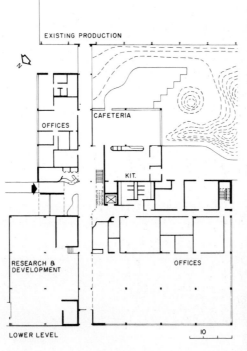

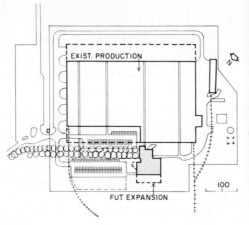

Housing administration, employee facilities and a research and development laboratory, the new building (at right in photo above) is an extension of the massive older plant seen at the left. All of the new facilities are related to a glass roofed corridor (photo left) which terminates at an outside wall (photo below) and in a production aisle of the plant (right), forming an unmistakable "heart" for the whole plant. A gate under the exposed duct (photo opposite page) allows employee facilities (located toward the production areas) to be isolated from the offices for night shifts.

10

The Federal Reserve Bank in Minneapolis has a complicated program rendered in unforgettable terms. Security operations which require protected facilities (about 60 per cent of the total square footage) are below the ground underneath a sloping plaza. Clerical and administrative operations are housed in an office block suspended from two great concrete towers. The catenary members which support the office floors are echoed in the curtain wall. Below the curve the glass stands forward; above it stands behind. For clean and strong architectural gesture, the likes of this solution have not been seen very often in recent years. Ask anybody in Minneapolis about the Federal Reserve building; if they draw a blank, then describe a catenary with your hand and they'll know what you mean. That fact in itself represents an achievement of sorts.

The architects' design commanded an unusual performance by the structural engineers. Most knew that it was possible to build an office building with a column-free span of 275 feet, but until then no one had actually done it, and few would quibble over the reported price tag that is above average. In concept the structure is simple but in practice it is something else. Two catenaries, one on either side of the building and 60 feet apart, support the major facades. These are rigid frames which in turn support the concrete slab floors. The tendency of the supporting towers at either end to topple inwards is checked by two 28-foot-deep trusses at the top of the building; the space in between them contains the mechanical equipment. One result of all these labors is a set of eminently flexible work spaces. Another result is the creation of a 2.5 acre public plaza sloping gently upward to a height of 20 feet above the entrance level of the building (see photo overleaf).

The original Federal Reserve Bank of Minneapolis, like many of the other banks in the system, was built in the early 20's and was a windowless, forbidding structure. Its architect, Cass Gilbert, described it as "a strongbox for the currency of the Northwest." The president of the Bank today echoes Gilbert's concern for security, but he also adds a new twist: "The responsibilit of the Bank to serve the financial community and the public requires openness and accessibility." This without question is an admirable intention, resulting in offices with a view, and a plaza for the general public.

Admirable, too, are the intentions behind the unabashedly glamorous form of the bank and the unusual structural system. Some of the manifestations and the perhaps large significance of all this good will become obvious.

FEDERAL RESERVE BANK OF MINNEAPOLIS. Architects: *Gunnar Birkerts and Associates*—project director: *Charles Fleckenstein; director of production: Vytautas Usas; director of field administration: Gunars Ejups; interiors: Barbara J. Bos.* Engineers: *Skilling, Helle, Christiansen, Robertson* (structural); *Shannon & Wilson, Inc.* (foundation); *Jaros, Baum & Bolles* (mechanical/electrical). Consultants: *Cerami and Associates, Inc.* (mechanical/electrical); *Geiger & Hamme, Inc.* (acoustical); *McKee-Berger-Mansueto, Inc.* (cost); *Arthur W. Dana & Associates* food operations); *Hubert Wilke, Inc.* (audio-visual). Landscape architects: *Charles Wood & Associates, Inc.* General contractor: *Knutson Construction Company.* Plaza Sculpture: *Charles Perry, Dmitri Hadzi, and Paul Granlund.*

Balthazar Korab photos

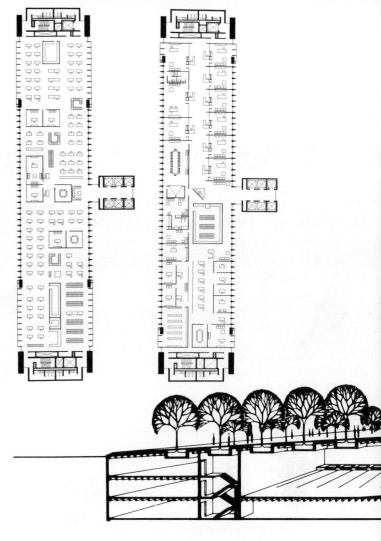

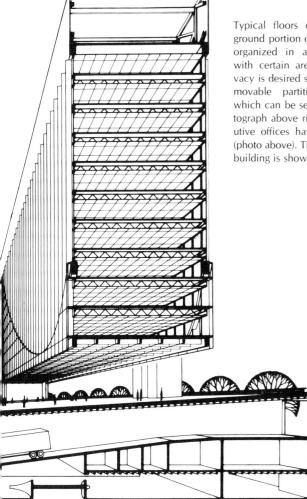

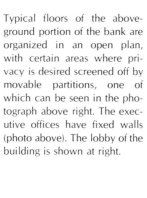

Typical floors of the above-ground portion of the bank are organized in an open plan, with certain areas where privacy is desired screened off by movable partitions, one of which can be seen in the photograph above right. The executive offices have fixed walls (photo above). The lobby of the building is shown at right.

The United States embassy in Tokyo has recently been designed by architect Cesar Pelli as part of a collection of buildings he designed as partner for design for Gruen Associates. Pelli's buildings are big, sleek, apparently light, and meticulously assembled, and the latest in the collection, the new embassy, is no exception. This replaces an older embassy, now demolished, on a lovely, garden-like site in the middle of the city. "It would be a good site anywhere," says Pelli, "but in Tokyo it is extraordinary." The building is set at an angle to the main axis of approach (which terminates at the gate in the lower right corner of the photograph opposite) in order to seem somewhat informally composed, and it seems as well to grow out of the hillside behind—a finely honed, eminently manmade object set in a natural context. The sides are the thinnest of curtain walls (made of anodized aluminum and mirror glass); and on the ends the concrete structure is revealed, like so much building cut from the stock of an elegant supplier.

Mitsuo Matsuoka photos

The State Department provided the architects with a very specific program which set strict limits on the amount of glass that could be used and which seemed to require a series of standard office spaces along double-loaded corridors. Any fears, though, that might have been generated by this requirement (which have resulted in some boring buildings in the past) have been assuaged by the result, which is a beautiful building that is in two parts, one high and one low, that together enclose the courtyard shown below.

Major spaces, when they occur, occur as multiples of the standard building bay, and often (as in the small photograph on the previous page) the structural system is allowed to remain intact. This is a direct answer to the seismic problem—and it also allows the structure to be clear. "Two systems play against each other," Pelli says, "enveloping skin and expressive structure." One admirable result of all this is a building that is at once commonsensical and elegant. "The design is straightforward," says Pelli. "We

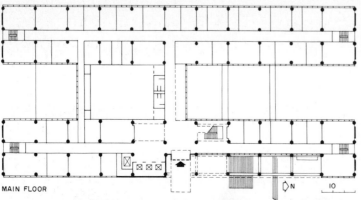

MAIN FLOOR   △N   10

strived for the simplest, most direct answer to each problem. This also resulted in an economical building." Pelli's whole approach to design, indeed, actively involves simplicity, directness, and (above all) do-ability. It is not just that do-ability is important if a building is to get built, according to Pelli, but that the questions of what can be done (and what really needs doing) are critical esthetic chasteners—reducing the realms in which the imagination takes fire, but allowing it to do so with more point.

UNITED STATES EMBASSY OFFICE BUILDING, Tokyo, Japan. Architects and engineers: *Gruen Associates of Los Angeles*—partner for design: *Cesar Pelli;* project designer: *Arthur Golding;* designer: *Fred Clarke;* project architect: *Rolf Sklarek.* Consultants: *Muto Institute* (soils); *Emmet L. Wemple* (landscape); *Richard Peters* (lighting); *Bolt, Baranek and Newman* (acoustical). Contractor: *Obayashi-Gumi.*

Mitsuo Matsuoka photos

5
Industrial Buildings

Granted that industrial buildings must be economical to build and maintain, and that the first design priority is operational efficiency, why can't they also be pleasurable to work in and enjoyable to look at? Must human values be ignored in order to maximize technological benefits? Of course not. On the pages which follow, projects are presented which go beyond economy and efficiency to satisfy aesthetic architectural criteria as well. Each of them has made use of an inexpensive idea or an intriguing design approach that could have application elsewhere.

It has long been the fashion to decry the architectural quality of the buildings designed for industry under the usual austere conditions. Indeed, the industrial clientele of the recent past placed both aesthetic and environmental qualities low in the order of priorities. The raising of priorities to current levels of emphasis for both environmental and aesthetic considerations has been impelled by a succession of strong influences.

First, with the rising power of organized labor and the increasing severity of employee compensation laws (with consequent upward pressure on insurance costs), the internal industrial environment improved in those aspects affecting health and safety. Thousands of complaints, ranging from fumes to radiation poisioning are received by the U.S. Department of Labor each year. Because of the mounting number of such complaints, Congress passed the Occupational Safety and Health Act of 1970 (Public Law 91-596). Under this law, which covers 57 million workers, occupational hazards are being identified and removed.

As a side benefit, demands for increasing precision in the manufacture of products brought about greater control of industrial atmospheres and lighting. Investment in both manufacturing and research buildings increased to meet the higher demands of both employees and products.

Another, more recent major influence has been the increasing sophistication of clients with large industries about the positive effects, on both productivity and public image, of those aspects of structure and building appearance which are more conventionally considered to be architectural. Those clients who had been through the experience of attempting in-house architecture and engineering found that, not only was the workload factor on in-house staff uneconomical, but an essential element of input from outside professional services was lacking. That input, over and above conventional, critical, analytical, and design services includes the spin-off of new ideas and technique normally acquired by professionals in private practice serving diverse clients.

The disciplines of the industrial milieu, nevertheless, continue to have their effect. And it has been in this milieu that the emerging practices of phased construction, systems building, and construction management have had their most searching trials.

The role of the architect as coordinator of the many disciplines involved in today's construction process is keyed to the preservation of the environment in which all men must live and work. This is not because the architect is either omniscient or inordinately arrogant. It is the simple fact that only architects have the breadth of viewpoint that enable them to consider all aspects of the process, from design through construction, and be an exponent of his or her clients' needs and desires. This is a role that may not be subverted by conflict of interest without peril to the whole process. It is the only profession in which the central thrust of training and endeavor is toward reaching the unencumbered goals of all concerned. Such architecture for industry has indeed been a proving ground for many such premises. The demands of clients for more than what are essentially simple enclosures have fostered many experiments in "off-the-shelf" architecture. Most of these have served only to demonstrate the poor performance of the compromise, and the industrial client now is almost universally converted to professional input, with all its disciplines and services.

Today, those who manage the building programs of industry, often themselves architects or engineers, feel they are best served by architects who understand that initial costs and operating costs are of utmost importance. Architects who manage to achieve the element of art as well (at absolutely no additional charge, of course) will undoubtedly be well received by this type of client, and garner a fair share of the constantly growing market.

The Southeast and Southwest regions of the country seem to be favored for industrial expansion. The second most preferred areas are the West and Midwest, although all regions of the country are expected to show marked increases in industrial building activity in the future.

There should be a unification of concerns between the architects and others involved in industry. Better planning means better functioning and working conditions, and is not just "hanging on the decoration" as industry seems to have long suspected. Aligning design to new client realizations may mean more of the architect's involvement in the process of what goes on inside the plant with resulting acceptance of efficiently running mechanisms as beauty in themselves. The projects shown on the following pages all illustrate the design considerations discussed here—and illustrate the individual architect's abilities to show that good planning can mean a long-term benefit to industry and the public alike.

1

The winner of a prestigous R. S. Reynolds Memorial Award, this Swiss industrial building, was cited more for its humanistic and environmental qualities than for its innovative use of aluminum. In its report, the Reynolds jury emphasized its pleasure at finding a well designed factory that takes both the exterior and interior human environment into account. Many aspects of the care in planning for an optimal working space are evident in the design. All production workers, for instance, are located on the second floor, where views outside are best. The open layout of manufacturing departments encourages a feeling of close interrelationship between employees in various areas.

Aside from the more intangible benefits of an insulating wall through which workers can keep in touch with the outside world, the architects noted some solid economic facts: "Complex investigation showed in this case that if all factors were considered—such as the ratio of floor area to perimeter, operation expenses, maintenance and installation costs—and if all these factors are weighted in an optimal solution, the price of such a curtain wall is no longer a disturbing factor and can be justified." Aluminum seemed a natural material to the architects for the lightweight cantilevered solar glass sunscreen which also serves as a maintenance platform and fire escape.

Although some of the technical concepts in this building may not be applicable in American industrial construction, there are obvious lessons in the way the building relates to its site. As more and more plants are built in rural areas, the designers would do well to consider the advantages of opening the walls to sunlight and natural vistas.

MASCHINENFABRIK HEBERLEIN AND CO. AG, Wattwil, Switzerland. Architects: *Professor Walter W. Custer, Fred Hochstrasser and Hans Bleiker.*

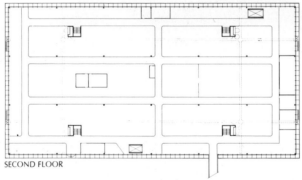

SECOND FLOOR

Maschinenfabrik Heberlein, one of the first buildings of an industrial complex being built near Zurich, has a clarity that is typical of the best European industrial building. Seen at night, above, the glowing facade seems a fully logical extension of the plan and wall details, left. The cantilevered glass and aluminum sunscreens, above left, are obviously important in controlling the effects of both sunlight and heat while still permitting a clear view for the workers of the nearby river and the alpine hills beyond.

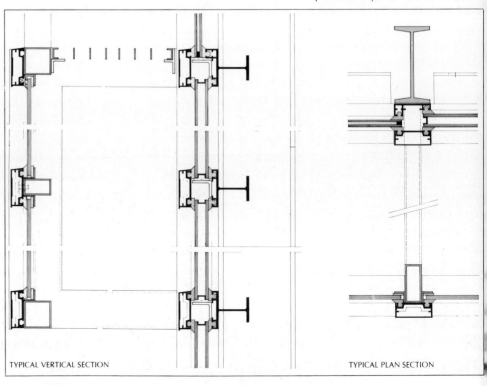

TYPICAL VERTICAL SECTION

TYPICAL PLAN SECTION

2

So often in industrial buildings the visitor's entrance, with severe chairs, aerial photos of branch factories on the wall and some back issues of trade magazines on a table, seems a forgotten corner of the plant. No one but the receptionist is there and the vitality of the production operations inside is certainly not expressed. Partly because of the very tight economic program for the Fagersta Steels building, but also because they wished to avoid a similarly dead reception area, Architects Bohlin and Powell made sure that the new reception area was thoroughly integrated with the rest of the facilities.

Furthermore, by making it a bold element in an otherwise severely straightforward building, the architects have provided a working pivot point around which the building always will revolve, no matter how much it expands. In this case the room serves many functions. Office and factory employees both may use it to enter each morning and to pass through on the way to lunch. Visitors have little trouble, of course, finding the entrance. Passersby, both day and night, have a landmark which becomes a living symbol. Thus the additional cost is more than justified by intangible benefits conferred upon employees and the community.

The real accomplishment is larger still, however. The architects have faced the problem of the low-budget industrial building, have extracted the humanistic aspects and have used them with great assurance to produce a building built of the most economical materials yet with great and enduring style. Which is—at low cost—a great deal indeed.

FAGERSTA STEELS INCORPORATED, Mountaintop, Pa.; Sponsoring agency: *Luzerne County Industrial Development Authority;* Architects: *Bohlin and Powell;* structural engineers: *Vincent B. Szykman, Inc.;* mechanical and electrical engineers: *Roushey Associates.*

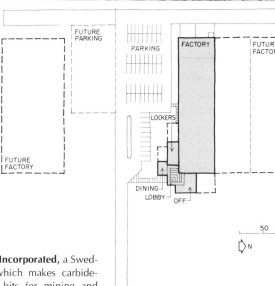

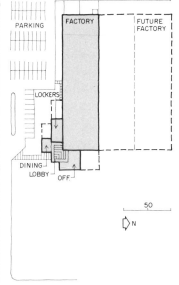

Fagersta Steels Incorporated, a Swedish company which makes carbide-tipped drilling bits for mining and heavy construction, needed a building which could expand easily to five times its original size. The design solution, above, with the sky-lit entrance lobby as the only unchanging element, makes it possible for every other element to grow as needed. The formal clarity of the scheme is apparent in the exterior photographs. The liveliness necessary to relieve such restraint is supplied by the solar gray acrylic roof which has varying degrees of transparency throughout the day. The indoor foliage and the lively banners, designed by Annie Bohlin, are always visible from the road, slightly higher than the building. Unpainted concrete block bearing walls and exposed steel beams and roof deck are the structural materials throughout the entire building. The floors in the office are carpet, in the lobby, brick pavers.

Frank Burnside Jr. photos

3

Although architects have been trained for many years to analyze the site thoroughly, how many really bother when designing an industrial plant? And there are those, of course, who see the building as a man-made object set into nature and so refuse to bother. But with "ecology" on everyone's lips today, it is a question which must be considered even when designing factories.

There are many advantages to modifying the building to fit the site rather than the other way around—as the Gordon Engineering Company complex shows. Using three identical structures (each involved in a separate phase of electronic component design and manufacture) connected by steps inside the links, Elroy Webber was able to respond to very subtle changes in grade without aggressive grading. Thus the building, although clearly not trying to blend with nature, seems far more sympathetic to its site than most factories ever do.

The economic advantages are also impressive. Grading costs include not only the initial shaping of the land, but the reapplication of topsoil and replanting. And the less the earth is moved, the easier that will be. Furthermore, water runoff problems, not always completely foreseen, can of course be minimized if nature's patterns are disturbed as little as possible. Finally, by keeping parking away from the building, as Webber did here, the effect of paved parking lots on groundwater conditions around the foundations is minimal. In this case, slightly more than five per cent of the total project cost was spent on site work and landscaping, yet the result seems very rich indeed.

GORDON ENGINEERING COMPANY, Wakefield, Massachusetts; Architects: *Elroy Webber Associates;* structural engineers: *Loomis and Loomis;* landscape design: *Elroy Webber Associates.*

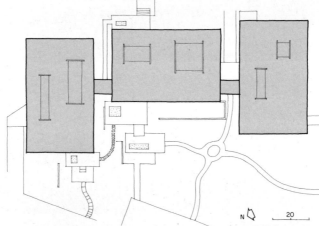

Jonathan Green photos

The Gordon Engineering Company's building is not only beautifully related to its site, but is an outstanding example of economic industrial building design. In order to meet package-builder prices—that were absolutely minimal—architect Webber chose to build three small identical buildings rather than one larger one. Short steel spans, simple masonry bearing walls, flexible mechanical equipment, low fire ratings all resulted from his decision. Seen from across the neighboring marsh, a bird sanctuary, above, the horizontality of the buildings is especially apparent. The terrace outside a conference room also helps to integrate building and site.

Cummins has continued to stand out as an exceptional client— even in the noteworthy architectural atmosphere of Columbus, Indiana. Having sponsored architects Roche and Dinkeloo's design for an impressive, prototype post office for Columbus in 1965 (as a public benefit), the company now has this monumental facility, and future plans (even more astounding) for their own offices, by the same architects. Since 1957, a foundation established by the company has paid the architectural fees for 18 public buildings in Columbus; it was recognized by the AIA, at the recent Atlanta convention, as the outstanding, professionally-related organization of the year. And the company's efforts here have certainly not gone unrewarded, in terms of public and employee relations.

On a large, heavily wooded site, Cummins comes as close to a "non-building" as possible. The visible, high storage-structure (photo right) occupies less than 10 per cent of the building's real area of 570,000 square feet, which is depressed to six feet below grade. Because of the massive roof structure required for cranes, parking space for 1400 cars (which would normally occupy an area, now forest, equal to the building itself) could be placed on top of the building with minimal extra reinforcement. Parked cars are shielded from the public road by sheets of opaque glass (photo top), which form a thin, visible "structure" separated from the ground by the recessed windows of the real building.

The usually amorphous spaces of production facilities are given visual orientation by these perimeter windows that face the meadow in front, the woods in back (over the low partitions of offices and cafeterias that line those walls) and a central, depressed court (photos, overleaf). And, they are given additional amenity by such details as wood-block flooring which provides resilience plus durability. Altogether, it is one of the best possible places to work — and to spend a good portion of a productive life. And it is a contribution to its environment.

WALESBORO COMPONENTS PLANT, Columbus, Indiana. Owner: *Cummins Engine Company.* Architect: *Roche and Dinkeloo Associates.* Engineers: *Pfisterer Tor Associates* (structural); *John Artieri* (mechanical/electrical); *Bolt Beranek and Newman, Inc.* (acoustical). General contractor: *F. A. Wilhelm Construction Co.*

4

Yukio Futagawa photos

Entrance stairs around the parking area (photo below) indicate the presence underneath of a much larger building than the immediately visible, storage bay (photos top and right). Apparently bucking the current trend away from glass enclosure for production areas, a small but conspicuous percentage of the real building is actually so sheathed. The remainder is below grade and is contained by retaining walls.

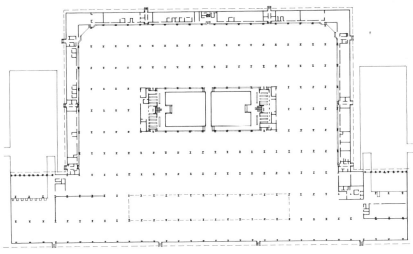

Access to roof-top parking is gained by bermed ramps to the left and right in the photo above. From this level, entrance stairs seem to lead into the surrounding forest or into a landscaped, central court, which is located halfway between the parking level and the production-floor below. The relation of that floor to the court can be seen in the lower photo, right; the raised gallery forms an area for lounging and is separated from the main floor by low walls—as are offices and cafeteria, located around the perimeter of the building (plan, right). The section (below) indicates the relationship of parking, grade and the production area, adjoining the cafeterias (second lowest level), which occurs at the corners of the building and are partially glass roofed.

Trucks enter the loading-dock areas (left and right in photo above) by roads that are ramped down to the depressed levels. Great care was taken to avoid cutting the existing trees which occupy much of the site. In the photograph at the upper right, the side of the building toward the forest can be seen. One of the glazed-roof cafeterias is in the distance.

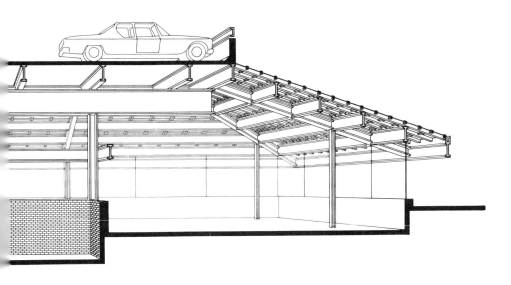

The interior of one of the two cafeterias (photo, above), located at the corners of the building toward the forest, gives the impression of a picnic arbor. The ambiance is furthered by "rustic" furnishings and sun umbrellas which serve a real function on bright days. In the top photo, the various materials of brick and woodblock paving, exposed concrete and brilliantly colored, glazed tiles are seen. Attention to detail is evident in the lighting and in the furnishing of the production areas (photo, right).

5

Chipper Machines and Engineering Company is located in a small-scale industrial park adjacent to one of Portland, Oregon's better residential areas, Oswego. Architect John Thodos hopes that his design will set a precedent for future industrial expansion in the area, and a general neighborhood acceptance of the new building should be an influence in that direction. The production space height and the 22,000-square-foot floor area—while not large by industrial standards—could have easily dominated the locale without the sensitive distribution of building mass that has occurred. Basic production is carried on in the high linear craneway along which ancillary shop and electronic areas are distributed. Office and ancillary spaces serve as a street buffer—as does the largely natural site. Another happy planning decision was the cladding of the building in wood: redwood exterior with cedar and hemlock finished interiors. The wood sheathing is compensated by the use of sprinklers and—while not a universally applicable industrial cladding—it is described by the architect to be adequate for this function and location. While furthering the cause of neighborhood congeniality, the cladding also provides an appropriate boost to the product manufactured: a wood chipping machine that removes the rough outside of logs and leaves rectangular shapes suitable for lumber production. Edmund Gurney, president of Chipper, invented the machine and emphasized its efficiency in producing a granulated matter suitable for lawn mulch—whereas older sawing methods produced largely scrap.

This building won a regional AIA Merit Award for *both* the architect and client. It is certainly one of the most "human" of industrial buildings to be seen.

CHIPPER MACHINES AND ENGINEERING COMPANY, Portland, Oregon. Owner: *Mrs. Marion Meade*. Architect: *John Thodos*. Engineers: *Pierson, Inc.—Jerry Estoup: principal-in-charge* (structural); *McGinnis Engineering, Inc.* (mechanical). General Contractor: *Triad Construction*.

Edmund Y. Lee photos

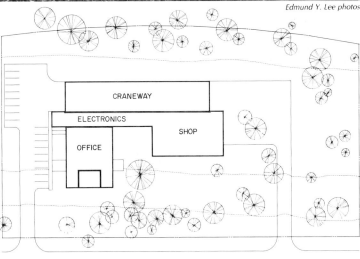

CRANEWAY

ELECTRONICS

SHOP

OFFICE

25

This plant houses the production of machines designed to rend logs suitable for lumber (photo left). Use of wood sheathing has expressed the nature of the business within—and coupled with a sensitive building massing—has shown that job resources could be brought compatibly closer to workers' homes.

Because of a talented in-house staff to develop design criteria, Westinghouse has been able to exactly determine the requirements that the corporation wants in each of its new facilities. Here, at Round Rock, Texas, the needs that were given to architects Caudill Rowlett Scott and Lockwood, Andrews & Neuman, included: a quick return on the initial investment, an interior environment that would facilitate good will between management and workers, and a positive impact on the neighboring community.

The architects produced a straightforward, square plan for the production spaces that accommodates the assembly aisles in the most efficient way and facilitated fast erection of the prefabricated, prepainted steel frame. Overlapping of the construction schedules allowed the building, of 240,000 square feet, to be completed in 18 months and for under the budget. To reduce heat transfer through the exterior walls of the totally air-conditioned spaces, the production area is windowless. The high mass required to house the crane bays is softened by a sheathing of weathering steel. Typical of this building type, the executive offices and employee facilities are contained in a separate, lower unit, but here that unit is visually integrated into the larger mass by being partially surrounded by it.

At the juncture of high and low elements, CRS introduced a glass enclosed court, which is simultaneously a relief from the windowless production spaces and a pleasant meeting ground for all levels of employees at the plant. Here, everyone has their lunches, coffee breaks and meetings, in an environment that is visually connected, but atmospherically isolated, from the sometimes harsh climate outside. Every effort has been made to produce a space that people will enjoy, and which can be viewed from both production and office spaces. Windows (which do not increase heat transfer from or to the outside) open industrial spaces and offices to the court.

WESTINGHOUSE STEAM AND GAS TURBINE PLANT, Round Rock, Texas. Owner: *Westinghouse Electric Corp.* Architects and engineers: *Caudill Rowlett Scott and Lockwood, Andrews & Newman* — project manager: *Ralph Carroll;* lead designer: *Frank Lawyer.* Interior and graphic consultant: *CRS Interior/Graphic-director: Jeffrey Corbin.* General contractor: *Warrior Contractors.*

6

Jim Parker photos

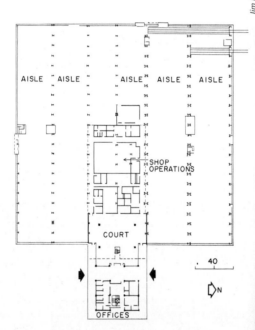

AISLE   AISLE   AISLE   AISLE   AISLE

SHOP OPERATIONS

COURT

40

N

OFFICES

ll employees and visitors
nter the massive building
nder the windows of the pro-
cting executive offices (photo
elow) and go to either the ex-
cutive lobby or the glass en-
osed court (right). This airy
pace is covered with an ex-
osed steel structure and
panned by exposed, round
ucts for air handling, which
so function as partial sun
reens. Plants and fountains
ve pleasant relief from the flat
rrounding landscape and the
nclosure of the heavy indus-
al spaces that can be seen
rough the glass walls.

7

Seiko's U.S. headquarters and watch assembly facility is located in the unfriendly environment of an established industrial park in Torrance, California. The surrounding structures largely reflect an expedient design approach antipathetical to the desired qualities of a stimulating working atmosphere—and a progressive corporate image. To counteract the new site's disadvantages, architects Kajima and Associates designed a building which can provide the desired qualities while standing up to its neighbors (despite its small 20,000 square feet). Torrance hopes that Seiko will serve as a model for future industrial development to come.

An early decision was the provision of a large percentage of open site with landscaping, and this will be largely continued in an anticipated doubling of floor area in the future. While the assembly area will expand horizontally, the office block will expand to a second floor to be added on the exposed steel framing without interruption of the ongoing first-floor operations. Because of this difference in projected expansion techniques and the proportionally large area of independently functioning office space required, there was no attempt to integrate manufacturing and headquarters operations into one building. An open central pedestrian spine is meant to provide a consolidation of feeling for office and factory worker alike. All must enter by one means and may meet at lunchtime or for meetings (middle photo, far right). All offices face the mirrored glass exterior and are arranged around a showroom whose exposed steel ceiling appropriately reflects industrial proximity. The factory building is built with "tilt-up" concrete panels and wood laminated beams. It can be expanded to the south.

U.S. HEADQUARTERS—SEIKO IN-STRUMENTS, INC., Torrance, California. Architects: *Kajima Associates—principal architect: Hayahiko Takase; project manager: Roosevelt Suzuki; project designer: Takeshi Hirose*. Engineers: *Tom T. Kamei Associates* (structural); *Wittler-Young, Inc.* (mechanical); *Charles M. Sloan* (electrical). Landscape architects: *Takasaki and Associates*. General contractor: *Oltman Construction Company*.

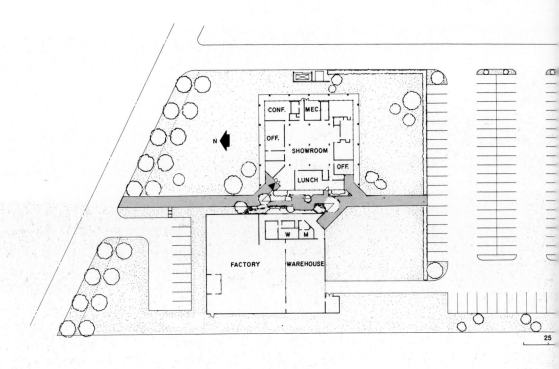

Mark Coppos photos

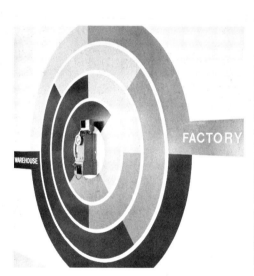

Office and manufacturing facilities are separated into two strongly contrasting but complementary volumes to establish an exemplary character for this plant in a highly impersonal industrial area. Generous landscaped open space will be maintained by future expansion of the office building to a second story added to exposed steel construction. All personnel enter on a single pedestrian spine which becomes a common meeting ground for gatherings and lunches promoting unity among all workers.

8

This plant for a unique client strongly exemplifies all three of the desirable qualities discussed in this study's introduction: neighborliness, a good place to work, and a forceful image for the product. And—while the client may be unique—Kahn and Jacobs' design principles seem widely applicable.

The Teaneck, N.J. site is a heavily wooded buffer between a residential neighborhood of single-family houses and a railroad track. The visual presence of the building's 60,000 square-foot-floor area is reduced by tree concealment, a healthy setback from the main road, and a break-up of mass achieved by articulation of the internal functions. An anticipated doubling of floor space will be achieved by a second story rather than by increased site coverage. Parking is conveniently distributed around the building in isolated clusters—not on one expanse of asphalt.

Dupont president Alvin Lindsay is an enlightened client who initially requested a building whose design qualities would be much more than a public facade. The results, shown here, have produced high worker morale, and Mr. Lindsay is proud to show visitors every corner of the new production space.

Project designer Der Scutt tells of a high degree of involvement with both the workers' interests and the production process, which is arranged in a work flow pattern. Perfumers, in semi-isolated "suites," make constant new fragrances which pass into sample preparation and on to production and storage. Each step was analyzed to produce efficiency and a personal identification by workers. An example of the latter is the provision of individual lighting seen at each work station in the sampling preparation area (opposite page, center).

ROURE BERTRAND DUPONT, INC., Teaneck, New Jersey. Architects: *Kahn and Jacobs—Project designer/interior designer: Der Scutt; project team: Thomas Burrow, Eunice Cahn. Engineers: Sigmond Roos (structural); M.P. Zacharius Associates (mechanical/electrical). General contractor: Wigton-Abbott.*

This plant is in harmony with a residential neighborhood and provides a happy working ambiance. The employee entrance (photo, left and closest plan arrow) is no less desirable than the public entrance (two photos, bottom). Work stations for samples (below) and production (right) are arranged for maximum employee identity.

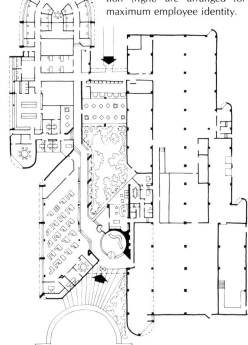

Norman McGrath photos

9

Architects Kivett and Myers successfully adopted a "background" approach to this mammoth Jefferson City, Missouri heavy manufacturing facility. Unlike the projects on the preceding pages, there was little question of the ability to visually reduce such a large bulk by segmenting the building into smaller parts. Big is big. Instead the architects chose to play the design to (and complement) an even larger scaled horizontal element: the 150-foot-high bluffs that contain the Missouri basin. A combination of dark coloration (natural rusting steel siding) and horizontal massing (the usual roof top mechanical equipment was depressed and vents are contained in the facade protrusions) produces the view from the Missouri State Capitol Building seen close-up in the center photo, far right. Fill, from a newly dredged lake, was used to raise the building only above flood levels.

By contrast, the interior of the new facility exerts itself in a forcefully concerted manner. A prime intent was oneness of all personnel who enter through a single means: a wide wood floored corridor past a cafeteria, other employee amenities, and offices. The office wing, whose two stories roughly equal one of manufacturing space, is integrated into the fabric of the total building. The production spaces are well ordered though vast, and wall graphics have been employed for visual relief and to furnish information about location—such as that over the main plant exit (photo, right). The exceptional designs are being considered for use in other Westinghouse facilities.

The windowless design is intended to facilitate a (currently problematical) climate-controlled interior. The wall sheathing is heavily insulated to produce a low heat transfer in this region of extreme temperature differential.

WESTINGHOUSE UNDERGROUND DISTRIBUTION TRANSFORMER PLANT, Jefferson City, Missouri. Owner: *Westinghouse Electric Corporation.* Architects: *Kivett and Myers.* Engineers: *Howard, Needles, Tammen & Bergendoff* (structural); *Holloway, Perkins & Eisman* (mechanical/electrical); General contractor: *J.S. Alberici Construction Company.*

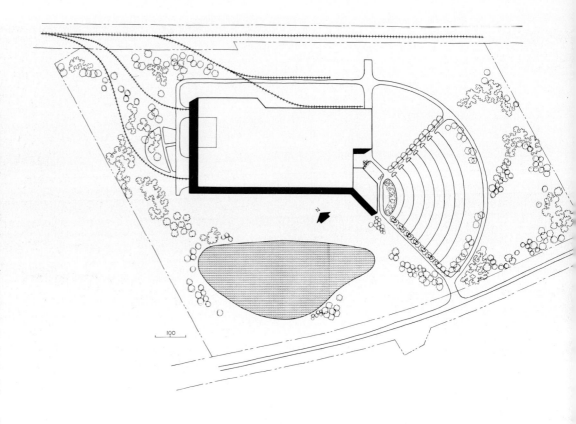

Paul Kivett photos

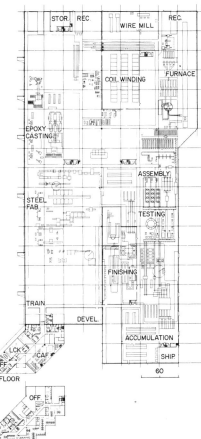

The Missouri State Capitol building is located nearby (just out of sight — to the left — in the top photo). The view of this new plant from the Capitol steps is seen in closeup (above), against the strong horizontality of 150-foot-high bluffs. All personnel enter through one means: a wide corridor in the two-story office area (lower left, in plan). Interior graphics are used to brighten production spaces, (photo left) supply information and provide a sense of location for workers. The facility produces electrical transformers for underground power systems and will have a good long-term effect on the country's over-all landscape.

10

This 600,000-square-foot Fogels-ville, Pennsylvania facility has been designed to hug a rural 160-acre site—and stand out at the same time. Certain elements have been chosen for visual emphasis, in line with the client's desire that the public be not only aware of, but induced to tour the full plant. The most prominent element contains the grain storage silos and two stainless steel kettles behind the 40-foot-high brewhouse windows (photo, upper right). The functions are clearly revealed and at the same time, the forms are reminiscent of the adjacent agricultural structures, here translated into red brick, concrete and glass. The walls of the lower parts of the building are visually relieved by brick recess details reflecting the rounded shapes of storage tanks (photo, opposite page, center) within. The rounding of exterior wall corners is derived from the silo shapes.

A happy collaboration between architects The Eggers Partnership and corporate production planners produced a plant closely related to the production process. One of the first design steps was preparation of a model of the facilities mechanism around which the form of the building was determined.

Schaefer's contribution to its Lehigh Valley location is multifold. The plant provides up to 400 jobs and produces 800,000 barrels of beer a year under extreme cleanliness requirements and with a high degree of automation benefiting consumer and worker alike. A strong emphasis on quality control produced the requirement for a large testing laboratory. Effluent is limited to that of gas or low-sulfur oil consumption. Used grains and hops become feed for farm animals and other by-products are similarly employed by the surrounding farms.

LEHIGH VALLEY BREWERY, Allentown, Pennsylvania. Owner: *F & M Schaefer Brewing Company.* Architects: *The Eggers Partnership—partner-in-charge: David L. Eggers; project designer: John B. Hayden.* Associated architects and engineers: *Sverdrup & Parcel and Associates.* Landscape architect: *M. Paul Freidberg.* General contractor: *J.A. Jones Construction Company.*

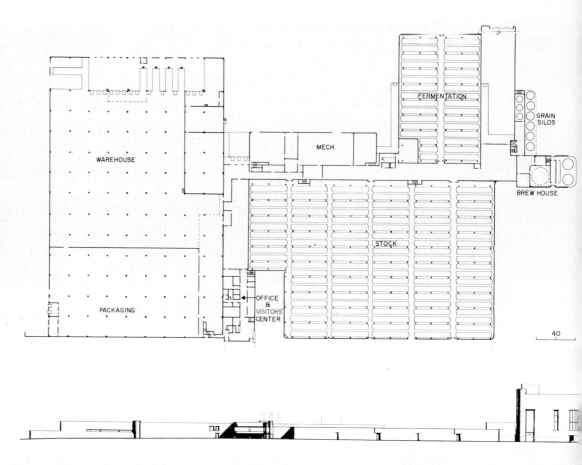

This large chemical production facility is located in a residential section of Memphis, Tennessee adjacent to the offices of architects Walk Jones + Francis Mah. The design involves a number of good-neighbor concepts.

Offices, production backup and employee facilities are contained in the cleanly detailed dark glass, steel framed building seen in the foreground of the photos. The bulk has been arranged for minimum visual obtrusion and is further broken up with the introduction of poured concrete stair towers outside the building envelope. Parking is concealed from the street by earth berms. By contrast, little attempt has been made to conceal the production facilities whose wiry appearance forms a sculptural counterpoint to the solid shape of the building. Visual treatment of exposed mechanical functions is reminiscent of Dow's program in Michigan (overleaf), and the reduced scale of elements here makes the approach fully compatible to residential proximity.

BUCKMAN LABORATORIES—PHASE ONE, Memphis, Tennessee. Owner: *Buckman Laboratories, Inc.* Architect: *Walk Jones + Francis Mah, Inc.*— project designer: *Francis Mah;* project architect: *Raymond Scott.* Engineers: *O. Clarke Mann, P.E.* (structural); *Griffith C. Burr* (mechanical). Contractor: *Harmon Construction.*

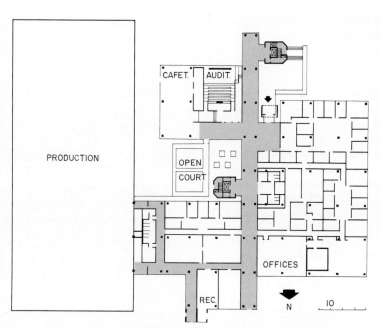

Otto Baitz photos

The use of perimeter skylights, white paint and colorful graphics has produced a cheerful environment for employees in this 60,000-square-foot Milwaukee, Oregon plant. Hubs for four-wheel-drive cars and winches are among the small metal parts produced. The 12-acre-site is located in an industrial area, but landscaping, saving of natural trees and orientation of windows toward unspoiled views have removed many usual shortcomings of such a location.

Architects Campbell, Yost and Grube designed the steel frame building for future expansion. Accordingly, the weathering steel exterior walls could not be used for bracing and are isolated from structural columns—facilitating the skylight locations. Offices and employee amenities are incorporated into the basic shed-type construction providing a unity to the building and a lack of the psychological separation of workers and management inherent in the "office wing" planning approach. The high ceiling in the cafeteria is a welcome result.

WARN INDUSTRIES, Milwaukee, Oregon. Architects: *Campbell, Yost and Grube and Partners—design partner: Richard Campbell; design assistant: Joe Macca*. Engineers: *Peterson Associated Engineers, Inc.* (mechanical/electrical); *Engineering Pacific, Inc.* (structural). General Contractor: *T&C Construction*.

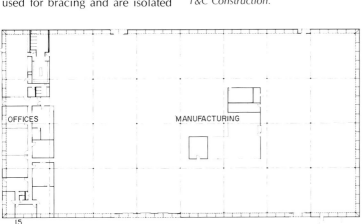

OFFICES   MANUFACTURING

15

SHOP

A straightforward steel structured loft building has been made a congenial place to work by the introduction of natural light, crisp white walls, pleasant views and a physical arrangement encouraging unity between management and employee. Unusual planning joined offices, facilities and production space under one roof.

C. Bruce Forster

13

The Dow Chemical Company's Midland Division comprises one of the world's largest chemical production complexes—occupying over 2,000 acres and 500 buildings. The plant celebrated its (and Dow's 75th anniversary in 1972 with a re-analysis of ongoing facility renewal and replacement procedures. Dow property manager Hugh Starks explains that the result was a desire for a strengthened procedural organization with a clear aim of making Dow's large physical presence compatible to workers, the public and neighbors (nearly 500 separate properties abut the plant).

Planners HOK Associates (Jamie Cannon, project manager and Frank Clements project designer) were commissioned to do a study of the best courses of action, and some remarkable implementations have occurred—with more to come. In line with a good neighbor policy, a large part of the Company's concern involved the plant's impact from the site perimeters, which had become deteriorated despite the proximity of downtown Midland (upper left in the plan) and the homes of Dow's top management. But even early concerns did not stop at the plant perimeters and one of HOK's first steps was the preparation of a "blight plan" of all nearby properties.

One of the first design assumptions was the sound acceptance of the major plant elements of tanks, piping, stacks and metal clad structures as visually interesting shapes without need of cosmetic coverup except for new light gray paint ot enhance sculptural qualities and lighten building interiors. The program has been a great success with workers (Dow realized the necessity of their people appreciating the value of all the present programs). Ground-level clutter became the target for basic design efforts, and the results can be seen in the section, opposite page. Typically the existing visual elements consisted of massive parking areas facing streets, chain link fence surrounding the whole site, overhead power cables, and the endless— but necessary—flow and storage of smaller portable equipment and supplies (photos, opposite page).

HOK's site perimeter recommendations involved removing as much parking as possible from the land between street and fence to a landscaped center strip of a new parkway created from two streets (point 3 on site plan). The old parking areas will become a bermed and planted zone to conceal the fence and ground level clutter and provide a green buffer to outside properties (as well as a visual base to the industrial sculpture above). Overhead power lines are to be buried. Fill for the berms comes from dredging of the old sediment ponds (7) which are being converted to naturally shaped landscaped lakes while continuing their old functions more efficiently. A new Overlook Park (6) will provide the view across the lakes seen in the night photo, opposite page.

Internally, efforts include organization of both existing visual and traffic pattern confusion, a unification of scattered research facilities into a campus area, a reorientation of the headquarters area (1) and a park strip along the river banks. A simultaneous 7.9 million dollar environmental protection program is being carried through. Dow's eventual aim is a zero effluent plant.

Today, Dow has gone further than some of their original goals. A downtown revitalization study is being prepared by HOK, and Dow is a catalyst in carrying through study recommendations. Implementation of city approach improvements (2) as well as plan recommendations along one road (5) may be put into physical form by the Midland Community Organization originating in HOK's study and set up to receive monies from foundations and find practical methods of carrying through on planning. Other programs are waiting normal cyclical renewal dates. Painting is done on a four-year rotating basis, and some burial of power lines may await required replacement dates. The Poseyville Road phase (4) is completed as planned (except for planting). The adjacent Dow-Corning plant had adopted a similar program by HOK—now largely implemented. With the backing of Dow General Manager Joe Temple, Dow's goal for a substantial carry-through on planning lies within the decade.

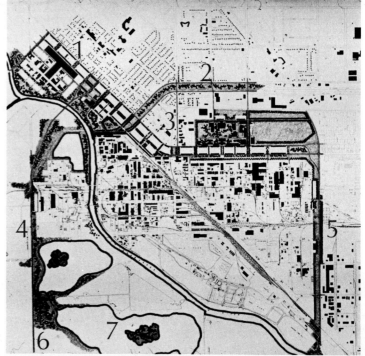

The view above is about to change. A section indicates the removal of parking and replacement by a planted earth berm concealing fencing and ground-level clutter. The full Dow program involves all areas of the plant. Shading on the plan indicates perimeter renewal. The aerial view shows the diversity of neighbors (foreground), the headquarters undergoing re-planning (center) and a sediment pond to become a lake.

14

The potential for providing architectural services in industry exists in almost every on-going plant maintenance program in the country. No one knows this better than HOK Associates—planners, landscape architects and civil engineers affiliated with architects Hellmuth, Obata & Kassabaum. In their precedent-setting visual improvement program for Dow Chemical Company in Midland, Michigan (see pp. 178 and 179 for description of this program), HOK Associates showed how reshaping a manufacturer's routine maintenance program could—without significantly increasing the budget—immensely benefit those who work in, live near, or pass by the giant Dow complex. (The bottom photo at the far right illustrates part of the Dow graphics treatment.)

The point is made again in the HOK Associates' visual improvement program for BP Oil Corporation in Marcus Hook, Pennsylvania (below).

Visual improvement in existing industrial plants is an idea that HOK Associates has been nurturing with some success in the years since the Dow Chemical experience. Currently, the firm is designing "visual improvement" programs for such companies as Exxon Company U.S.A., Union Carbide, PPG Industries, Allied Chemical, Ingersoll-Rand, Phillips Petroleum, ERDA and FMC Cor-

poration. In all, HOKA clients have, in one five-year period spent $10,000,000 to improve plant-community interface, worker conditions, and company image at a time when the nation's communities expect increased environmental concessions during industrial expansion.

One of HOKA's most recent visual improvement projects, (page at right), was inspired by the success of the Dow Chemical work. The adjacent Dow Corning plant took advantage of a city program to widen Saginaw Road—which forms a main, common boundary of both Dow plants—to establish a major upgrading of its own. The work included a landscaped buffer along 3,270 linear feet of arterial street frontage, redesign of the plant's internal vehicular circulation system, reconstruction of parking areas, installation of new light standards, an underground sprinkler system, and application of a coordinated color scheme throughout the plant.

Preliminary development work, including site analysis, activity survey, visual impact analysis, and programming was accomplished in late 1973, and the construction phase was completed in 1974 at a cost of $1,020,000.

Until 1974, this area had severe functional and environmental problems. Parking areas were unpaved and provided poor

circulation. In fact, the parking was scarcely separated from the arterial street (see photo, top right).

The HOK Associates solution first reorganized the plant frontage. Earth berms up to five feet high along Saginaw Road were added to screen the parking lots from the passersby, and soften the building profiles. The parking lots themselves were redesigned for better internal circulation, and paved. Curbs and gutters were added, and turnaround areas were located at the main entrance and medical building. The total number of parking spaces remained substantially unchanged. High maintenance landscaping—flower beds and trees unsuited to an industrial setting—were replaced with a combination of deciduous and evergreen trees.

One of the five original traffic access points from Saginaw Road was shifted to coordinate with internal street improvements planned for the Dow Chemical plant across the street, and a sixth traffic way was added to facilitate access to the northernmost parking lot. A random mix of plant color was replaced by a new scheme of earthtone hues. Production structures were painted a uniform gray to provide a dramatic backdrop for the brick office buildings in the foreground.

Only a small portion of the total cost at Saginaw went to actual "beautification"—many improvements, such as replacing light fixtures and paving the parking lots, would have been carried out as part of maintenance.

These design techniques can, of course, be best used at older plants. The opportunity to carry out a series of self-contained projects is attractive from the corporate standpoint since improvements can be implemented over several years within normal maintenance/plans and expense bud-

gets. Most master plans of this nature developed by HOK Associates are in the five-year range. (Dow Chemical's program is a 10-year plan).

In their visual impact analyses, HOK Associates recognizes that most plants affect five viewer groups:
■ The casually interested expressway traveler usually sees the installation at high speed and in the context of an industrial corridor.
■ The neighboring community will see the plant more often, at moderate speeds along certain peripheries. This group has an environmental and economic (tax base) regard for the plant.
■ The immediate neighborhood sees the plant from a stationary position and in great detail. At the very edge of the plant, this group has the same broad environmental and economic interests as the community, with the added economic interest of the plant's impact on property values.
■ Visitors to the plant see it at low speeds and have a need for orientation information.
■ The employees of the plant see it from a nearly stationary viewpoint, and have a constant need for information about the facility and safety. This group constitutes the plant's chief viewer group and can be its greatest proponent in the community.

SAGINAW ROAD DEVELOPMENT PLAN, Midland, Michigan. Owner: *Dow Corning Corporation.* Landscape architects, planners and civil engineers: *HOK Associates, Inc.*—project team: *Jamie Cannon, Franklin Clements, and Gerry Berutti.* Contractor: *Bay Landscaping.*

BP OIL CORPORATION, MARCUS HOOK, PENNSYLVANIA. Landscape architects, planners and civil engineers: *HOK Associates, Inc.*—project team: *Jamie Cannon, Terry Harkness, Ron Stup, Paul Henderson, Debbie Fitzpatrick.*

Normal maintenance of giant tanks (shown before and after) at the Marcus Hook, Pennsylvania location of BP Oil Corporation provided an opportunity to identify equipment easily for workers, and at the same time promote the company's position in industry to outsiders. (One might assume something about the size of a company with at least 500 tanks, for example.)

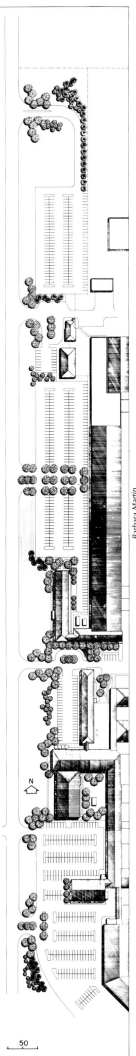

Barbara Martin

Barbara Martin

Barbara Martin

The Saginaw Road project area consists of 21.1 acres, a strip of road frontage with an average depth of 280 feet. The site contains office and production facilities, medical building, clock room, cafeteria, research building, and parking for 1500 employees.

15

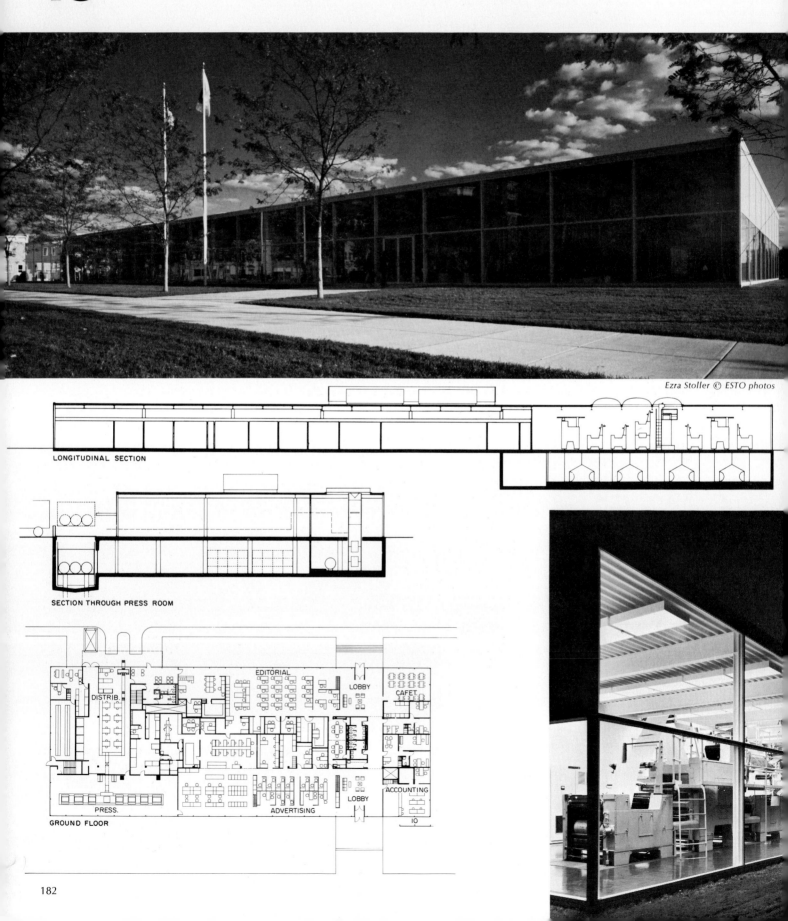

Ezra Stoller © ESTO photos

LONGITUDINAL SECTION

SECTION THROUGH PRESS ROOM

GROUND FLOOR

DISTRIB.

EDITORIAL

LOBBY

CAFET.

ACCOUNTING

LOBBY

ADVERTISING

PRESS.

10

Relatively few businesses of any kind live long enough or achieve sufficient eminence to justly be called "civic institutions." *The Republic,* a hundred-year-old Columbus, Indiana daily *is* a civic institution. When owner-publisher Robert N. Brown decided to move and build again, he settled on a prime, downtown site opposite the city courthouse. He commissioned Skidmore, Owings & Merrill (Myron Goldsmith, partner-in-charge) with whom he had worked before, because he is an owner who cares and because Columbus is a city that cares. Delicately framed and detailed in light steel and sheathed in tempered glass, the finished building has a decidedly "non-industrial" look. The decision to use large and vulnerable expanses of glass was not taken without considerable thought. A newspaper office, after all, is frequently the target of people with grievances both real and imagined. But because of the owner's confidence in his community and his conviction that a newspaper press is an exceptionally handsome piece of industrial design, the building was

largely enclosed with glass. As a result, much of the journalistic process is continuously visible. "Few other industries," says Brown, "can do this with such impact."

The program, drafted jointly by owner and architect, called for general office and editorial space in addition to press and composing rooms. By floating the press on a special pad with footings independent of the main foundation, vibration through the building is minimal. By isolating the press acoustically behind a glass wall, the office spaces are quiet even during the daily press run which lasts about an hour. Across the glass barrier, the sound drops from approximately 90 decibels to a faint, scarcely audible rumble.

Lithographic offset printing does not generate any significant contaminants so special pollution control devices are not required. Normal newspaper wastes — paper, ink, silicone treated wrappers — are hauled away under contract. There is no incineration on the site.

The building employs single, and multizone air conditioning units with ceiling diffusers and floor grilles at the perimeter walls. Mechanical spaces are located in the partial basement.

The owner does not anticipate major expansion. The new building was oversized by the architects to accommodate some natural growth. If unanticipated expansion occurs in future, it will probably be in the form of a new press room to be located elsewhere on the site. For this reason, the architects planned one discrete entity.

The new building for "The Republic" is an important part of the city's downtown renewal plan (also by Skidmore Owings & Merrill) that will soon include a two-block shopping mall. The architects kept the profile of the new plant as low as possible in deferenct to historic Bartholomew County Courthouse which stands just a block to the north — and is reflected gracefully in the new building's long glass wall.

THE REPUBLIC, Columbus, Indiana. Architects and engineers: *Skidmore, Owings & Merrill* (Myron Goldsmith, partner-in-charge; George Hays, project manager; Jin H. Kim, senior designer; George Larson, interior design; Philip Thrane, job captain). Contractor: *Dunlap Construction.*

16

On a 74-acre site outside Los Angeles, A. C. Martin and Associates have planned and designed a headquarters and manufacturing facility for the Parker Hannifin Corporation which designs and builds components for the aerospace industry. The 4-building facility encloses some 300,000 square feet and is planned for incremental expansion as production requirements change. To provide this flexibility, the architects designed a moment-resisting frame composed of open web steel trusses supported on 12-inch diameter pipe columns laid out on a 60-foot-square grid. Infill panels are lightweight, tilt-up concrete with a sand-blasted finish. The panels are demountable in the event of expansion. The open webs of the trusses are glazed along the outside walls to admit daylight. Costs were wintin the budget—almost twice the per-square-foot cost for the office and administrative areas as for the manufacturing spaces.

The client was aware from the beginning that what he needed was a factory. But he was convinced that within his budget, a pleasant level of employee comfort and

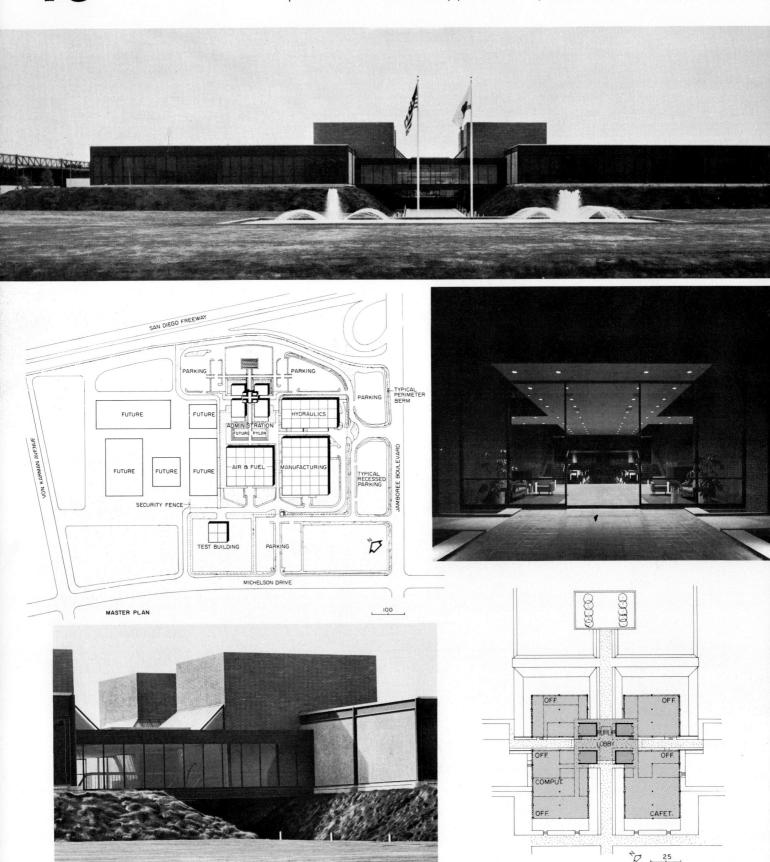

MASTER PLAN

amenities could be achieved. He was right. At reasonable costs and within a fixed structural system, the architects have provided a surprising richness. The buildings are grouped in a campus-like arrangement around a landscaped court. Parking areas are screened with earth berms. The steel detailing is consistent and surehanded. Added richness is provided by the use of narrow bands of color accents—blue at the fascia, red to outline the infill panels (photos below). A handsome sequence of signs identifies each part of the complex and

marks the routes between buildings. Berms are also used by the architects to screen the parking areas and to soften the effect of the encircling fence required by government security regulations.

Because the firm is involved in research and testing, certain flammable chemicals and volatile fuels are in more or less frequent use. Operations that require the handling of such materials are largely confined to a deeply bermed chamber at the south end of the site. The industrial park in which this building is located placed deed restric-

tions in its leases that established upper limits for industrial noise. In order to comply with these restrictions, the architects located the noisiest test equipment in this same bunker. Inside, a network of filter traps protects against hazards created by accidental spillage of hydraulic oil or other troublesome liquids.

On the assumption that a building's quality affects the performance of those who use it, Parker Hannifin was willing to make a substantial, long-term investment in its people and its product.

A large reflecting pool graces the main approach and the twin fountains and flagpoles reaffirm the plan's axial symmetry. Major expansion will occur in the form of a new building cluster to the west of the existing complex (see master plan).

PARKER HANNIFIN CORPO-RATION, Irvine, California. Architects and engineers: *Albert C. Martin & Associates* (*John Day*, partner-in-charge; *W. Jay Smith*, project director; *Michael O'Sullivan*, project designer; *Aram Tatikian*, job captain. *Bill Huddleston*, structural engineer; *Don Teske*, electrical engineer; *Tony Tang*, civil engineer; *John Swiatnicki*, interiors; *Robert Morgan*, graphics; *Vince Walsh*, estimator); soils engineer: *Moore & Tabert*; landscape architect: *Erikson, Peters & Thom*; contractor: *Robert E. McKee, Inc.*

SYSTEM

17

Carroll's tobacco factory has been a familiar landmark in Dundalk since its founding in 1824. In 1967, after numerous modernizations, the company's directors reluctantly abandoned the old site and purchased thirty acres just outside the city. They commissioned Michael Scott & Partners (Ronald Tallon, partner-in-charge) to design a new facility—a facility that would provide the comfortable, hygienic surroundings necessary to contemporary, heavily automated tobacco processing. The architects, after visiting new tobacco factories in various countries, prepared the drawings for the building shown in the photographs below.

Efficient operation and worker comfort were prime requisites. Because the business is competitive and the technology subject to periodic improvement, flexibility was also important. The Scott design addresses itself to all these needs. The entire four-acre structure is fashioned by the repetition of a single structural unit: a steel bay with a clear span of 67 feet 6 inches in both directions. The bay is framed out above with steel roof trusses 7 feet 6 inches deep—a depth suffi-

Though interior spaces vary widely in finish and function, the 67-by-67-foot structural bay is legible throughout. Parking for employees is at the site perimeter.

P. J. CARROLL & COMPANY, LTD., Dundalk, Ireland. Architects and engineers: *Michael Scott and Partners* (Ronald Tallon, partner-in-charge; Patrick Reeves, assistant architect; Charles Jenkins, mechanical engineer; Lawrence Kyne, electrical engineer). Structural consultants: *Ove Arup and Partners;* quantity surveyor: *Seamus Monahan.*

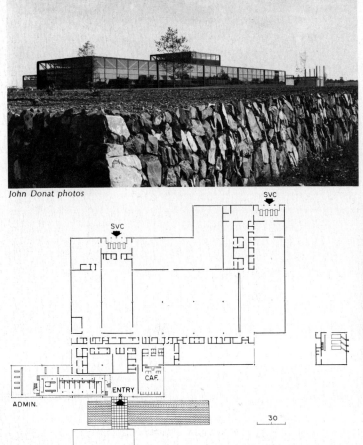

John Donat photos

cient to house and distribute all the complex mechanical and electrical services the factory requires. The whole structure is fully sealed and air conditioned.

Expansion will be in 5000-square-foot increments to be located as functional requirements may dictate. This flexibility, inherent in the basic planning, strongly influences the building's appearance inside and out. The modular bays are clearly readable and do not lose their definition whether the infill panels are grey brick in the processing areas or bronze glass in the offices.

The structure meets the ground precisely, but around the building the land undulates gracefully to create a series of barely perceptible swales. Seeded with grass and lightly spotted with trees, these generous park areas are an amenity to be enjoyed by owners and employees alike.

Visitors to the Dundalk factory approach over a bridge that spans a generous reflecting pool. Rising up from this pool, like a welcoming sentinel, is a tall, three-shafted, stainless steel abstract. Elsewhere in the building, tapestries, canvases and sculp-

tures by leading Irish artists express the company's desire to broadly identify the arts with industrial enterprise.

Rationally planned and efficiently assembled out of simple, preformed parts, the Dundalk plant uses the coherent, international language of industrial building and uses it well.

The architects express confidence that the new Carroll factory will be one of the most modern tobacco processing plants anywhere for many years to come, and their results justify their confidence.

18

The Hewlett-Packard Company, which produces electronic equipment in locations around the world, has through the years been quietly demonstrating its commitment both to quality working conditions for its employees, and to the enhancement of communities that accept its plants.

The plant shown here is located in Santa Rosa in northern California, on a 190-acre site. It is located in an area zoned for light manufacturing, but because the site is part of a residential development, the architects—John Carl Warnecke & Associates—recommended that the owner forego a preferred hilltop location in favor of buildings that step down the slope. A substantial benefit of doing so was to move the adjacent parking—and more importantly, the parking lot lighting—to a position that could not affect the residential community.

The overriding planning considerations of environment, employee satisfaction, and readily adapted manufacturing space are neatly realized in this project, the first phase of which includes the two buildings shown, the power plant, and parking. Eventually, the total enclosed area in eight buildings will comprise one million square feet, with parking for 4000 automobiles.

These buildings were competitively budgeted and consistent with the client's strict cost limits. The client's employee-per-square-foot ratio of 1:200, and "activity sheets" filled out by employees, helped determine the horizontal and vertical modules of the building. Two standard modules were found: a small planning module 5 feet square, and a large structural module 40 feet square. The vertical module is based on human floor-to-ceiling requirements, and the necessary mechanical systems located in interstitial space created by the use of deep trusses in two directions. The truss arrangement has the added benefit

of minimizing vibration and deflection, important in a building where much of the manufacturing is done under microscope.

The walls of the building are poured concrete with exposed local aggregate; stuccoed duct shafts are placed vertically at intermittent points along the building perimeter to exhaust the clean rooms. Air flows from the clean rooms down to the basement; it is then cycled up to the rooftop pollution scrubbers in these outside shafts. Keeping this ductwork and the service cores at the edge of the building gave the client the wide-open and flexible work spaces that were required for work and a view of the outdoors for all the workers.

The roof configuration resulted from the desire to conceal mechanical equipment. The material is orange clay tile. The stuccoed canopies that surround the buildings, and the roof overhangs, were dimensioned and positioned after careful sun studies documented the position of the sun at hour intervals during three seasons of the year. The data helped the architects determine the different size sun control canopies needed at various locations of the building. At points of future expansion, sections of the canopy can be easily removed without major structural modifications.

HEWLETT-PACKARD MICROELECTRONICS PLANT, Santa Rosa, California. Owner: *Hewlett-Packard Company.* Architects: *John Carl Warnecke & Associates—project designer: Edward M. Tower; project manager: Thomas W. Mulvey; interior designer: Jean B. Coblentz.* Engineers: *Nishkian, Hammill & Associates, Inc.* (structural): *Donald Bentley and Associates* (mechanical/electrical); *George S. Nolte and Associates* (civil); *Harding, Lawson & Associates* (soils). Landscape architects: *Michael Painter & Associates.* Consultants: *Fitzroy/ Dobbs* (acoustics); *Planned Warehousing Ltd.* (materials handling). General contractor: *Haas & Haynie Corporation.*

Robert Brandeis

Merg Ross

MULTI-PURPOSE

LOADING

BUILDING NO. 2
SECOND FLOOR

CAFET.

40'

N

LOBBY

CENTRAL PLANT

MULTI-PURPOSE

NOISE

BUILDING NO. 1
FIRST FLOOR

ALKS

RECREATION

PHASE ONE

PARKING

RECEPT. & TRAINING

N

150

Outdoor recreation area courts
were created between the
buildings. Natural walkways
are also included in site
improvements. Two
cafeterias—one on either
side of the main spine—are
located in two of the linkage
portions of the buildings.

12'-0"

5'-6"

17'-6"

12'-0"

8'-6"

20'-6"

12'-0"

TYPICAL CONDITION

6
Industry-Related Buildings

In this final chapter, there are a group of utilitarian buildings that are similar because they are necessary to the performance of often "heavy duty" tasks. Still, they are not typical factories that produce commercial products. They are waste treatment plants, power houses, warehouses, and research centers—and even a winery and a printing plant.

All of these buildings share the need for particularly thoughtful design because of their unique programs and specialized natures. Ironically, they belong to a building type that has often been the least considered on a visual level—often the ugly stepsisters of other new construction. But—just as the owners of factories are discovering—thoughtful design can produce a good appearance at little or no extra cost. And a good appearance will pay big dividends in gaining public acceptance of such projects when proposed, in the users satisfaction and in ongoing neighborhood relations.

An example of the specialized expertise that is required for each of the various kinds of industry related buildings, the following excerpt from recent article by ARCHITECTURAL RECORD associate editor Barclay Gordon explains some background to planning buildings for waste management: "The stream of municipal solid waste is extremely heterogeneous. It includes some of most everything: metals, plastics, wood, glass, textiles paper, food and yard waste. In Madison, Wisconsin two years ago, it included a live mortar shell and

n New York, three crates of live lobsters. Though
he potential salvage value in the waste stream has
ong been recognized, until recent years both the
ecovery technology and the economic incentive
ave been lacking. Now, both are developing
apidly. Subsidiaries of a number of technically
oriented corporations (Monsanto, Union Carbide,
Raytheon, American Can, Occidental Petroleum,
and others) are developing proprietary systems for
esource recovery—systems that shred, sort, and
eparate out valuable materials (principally glass,
errous and non-ferrous metals) for resale to second-
ry users. This is the "front end" of the waste
management concept, and 30 or more such systems
re now offered in the United States. After initial
orting in an air classifier, the light fraction (paper
roducts and other light organics) can be cleansed
f further impurities, reshredded to smaller size,
and used as fuel (either alone or in combination
ith fossil fuels) to generate electricity or steam.
his energy recovery potential is the 'back end' of
olid waste management. 'Front end' systems now
em economically attractive only in regions that
generate at least 750 tons of solid waste per day
opulation 350,000), and b) pay upwards of seven
ollars per ton for conventional disposal. When
e 'back end' can also be made to produce revenue,
e seven-dollar floor can drop to under four
ollars." Clearly, the buildings on the following
ages could not have been built without the help
experts.

WASTEWATER TREATMENT FACILITIES, WEST PLANT

1

For years this site in Fitchburg, Massachusetts, at the headwaters of the Nashua River, served as a sludge-holding pond for paper wastes from local mills. When it was drained, a 10-foot-thick blanket of wet pulp remained and had to be removed prior to construction. The stream that fed the pond was rechanneled to the edge of the site. What remained was a narrow site, depressed at one end, and bounded on two sides by water.

Architects Johnson-Hotvedt, working with engineers Camp Dresser & McKee, devised a diagonal process flow pattern in response to the site geometry and let the building fall logically, at the end of both the flow and the site. Because the process treats industrial wastewater, chiefly from two papermills, the engineers selected an activated carbon treatment system. The heart of this treatment system is a nest of 12 tall, granular carbon filters. The architects enclosed these filters in a weathering steel structure that reflects the diagonal site geometry both in plan and elevation. The pattern of the X-bracing was used to produce glazed openings in the siding that expose the nested carbon cylinders and admit natural light in large doses. Other materials were selected with a view toward durability and easy maintenance: glazed block for interior partitions and seamless epoxy flooring.

The West Fitchburg plant is a simple but convincing argument for architect/engineer cooperation in this neglected building type. Working in tandem, they achieved together what neither might have achieved alone.

WASTEWATER TREATMENT FACILITIES, WEST PLANT, Fitchburg, Massachusetts. Engineers: *Camp Dresser & McKee, Inc.* Architects: *Johnson-Hotvedt —Robert Pillsbury, designer.* Contractor: *Fontaine Brothers.*

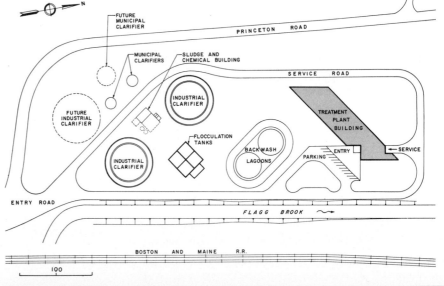

Chemical
Delivery ←
Sludge
Pick-Up ←
Visitor
Parking ↑
Receiving ↑
Carbon
Delivery ↑

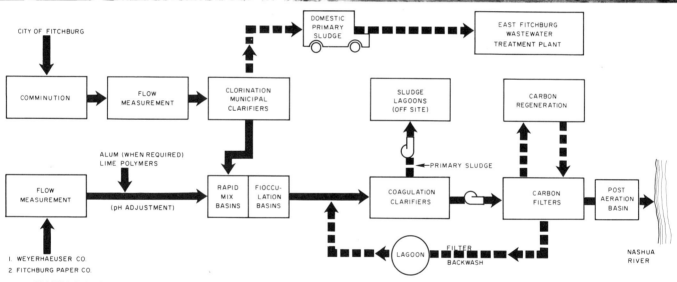

CITY OF FITCHBURG

COMMINUTION → FLOW MEASUREMENT → CLORINATION MUNICIPAL CLARIFIERS

DOMESTIC PRIMARY SLUDGE

EAST FITCHBURG WASTEWATER TREATMENT PLANT

ALUM (WHEN REQUIRED) LIME POLYMERS

FLOW MEASUREMENT

(pH ADJUSTMENT)

RAPID MIX BASINS | FLOCCU-LATION BASINS

SLUDGE LAGOONS (OFF SITE)

CARBON REGENERATION

←PRIMARY SLUDGE

COAGULATION CLARIFIERS → CARBON FILTERS → POST AERATION BASIN

1. WEYERHAEUSER CO.
2. FITCHBURG PAPER CO.

LAGOON

FILTER BACKWASH

NASHUA RIVER

PROCESS FLOW DIAGRAM FOR WEST FITCHBURG WASTEWATER TREATMENT PLANT

This 15.3 MGD facility is part of a two-plant system for the Fitchburg region. Here at West Fitchburg, industrial wastewater will be processed using an advanced wastewater treatment for removal of organic solids. After passing through flocculation basins, the wastewater passes through the carbon filters which are operated in parallel even during backwashing and carbon regeneration cycles.

This physical/chemical process was selected over more conventional treatment because it achieves a better effluent quality and better color removal. Together with the East Fitchburg facility, this plant makes a measurable regional contribution toward the planned cleanup of the Nashua River.

WATER POLLUTION CONTROL PLANT AT PLATTSBURGH

2

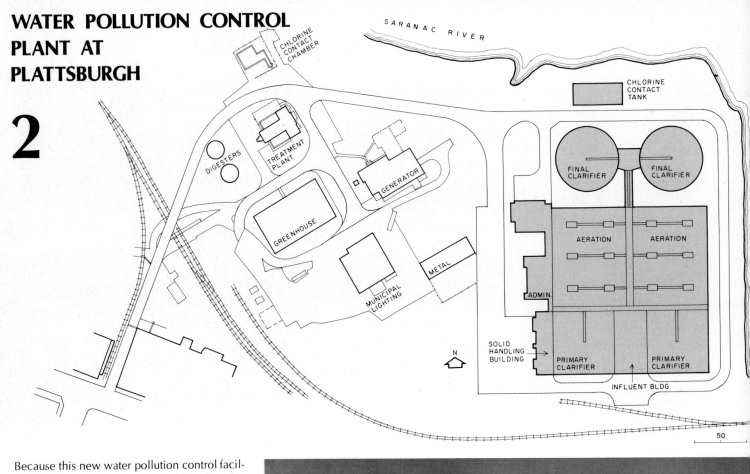

Because this new water pollution control facility is located adjacent to one of Plattsburgh's nicest residential neighborhoods and also next to a popular boating and recreational area, unusually high esthetic standards were adopted for its design. Engineers O'Brien & Gere and architects Macknight-Kirmmse worked with a tight site to produce a compact and orderly solution that masses the principal enclosures into a few powerful, concrete forms. The exteriors are board-formed, cast-in-place concrete, sealed and left natural in color. The roof structure is a waffle slab with all piping and ductwork left exposed and color-coded. Finishes throughout are modest.

The basic treatment process for this 16 MGD facility, which serves not only the city of Plattsburgh but a branch of the State University, a nearby Air Force Base and several local industries as well, includes pre-treatment, primary clarification, secondary treatment, final clarification and chlorination prior to discharge of the effluent into the Saranac River and Lake Champlain. The dewatered sludge is trucked to a nearby landfill.

The design input and architectural quality present in this facility have not gone unnoticed. Last year, Plattsburgh's water pollution control plant received awards from both the New York State AIA and the American Concrete Institute.

WATER POLLUTION CONTROL PLANT, Plattsburgh, New York. Engineers: *O'Brien & Gere*. Architects: *Macknight-Kirmmse—R.T. Kirmmse, partner-in-charge, William Slivers, project architect.* Contractor: *McElwee Courbis Construction, Inc.*

Pre-treatment (1) consists of coarse screening, comminution and grit removal. Primary clarification (2) follows during which 90 per cent of the settleable solids and over 50 per cent of the suspended solids are removed by gravity. The sludge is then stored for later dewatering by centrifuging. Aeration (3) is the next step in the wastewater flow and during six hours in the aeration tanks, organic materials undergo bacterial decomposition in the presence of oxygen. Sludge from the aeration tanks is then channeled into secondary clarifiers (4) where 35 per cent of the remaining suspended solids are removed. The treated clear liquid then flows into chlorine contact tanks (5) prior to its release.

Joseph Molitor photos

3

Processing, storage and retail sales are combined in this main building of the Sonoma Vineyards north of San Francisco. Although industrial buildings are rarely open to the public, the California wine industry typically promotes itself by inviting the public to see the wine making process—and to enjoy the popular event of wine tasting. Not only is this building open for public touring, but by virtue of its outdoor amphitheater, it provides an unusually dramatic setting for performing arts. Thus, a building that was needed for purposes of private enterprise has become a prestigious community asset as well.

The symmetrical, cruciform plan (right) of interior wings and exterior quadrants provided the most direct solution, in this case, to the private-public needs of the client—functional spaces define, at no extra cost, the pleasing public spaces. For instance, one of the exterior quadrants forms the main entrance; another quadrant, the amphitheater. The third quadrant is the service entrance, the fourth, processing space (grape crushing is done outdoors, and the product is pumped to the fermentation tanks inside).

The total building area of 27,500 square feet is broken down into four 100-by-50-foot wings that intersect in a 50-foot square containing the second-level wine tasting room and the third-level offices.

Construction is tilt-up exposed aggregate concrete bearing walls, 40 feet high at the center. Laminated fir beams span side to side. The insulated metal roof has a baked enamel finish.

Although not air-conditioned, the fermentation and storage rooms (photos far right) are cooled satisfactorily by "leaked" cool air given off by the refrigerated fermentation tanks. Also, at evening, when the outside air is cooler, doors are opened in the lower sections of the heavily insulated building, and a natural chimney effect vents any accumulated warm air at the top of the building.

A skylight in the center section of the winery brings light into the redwood-finished tasting room and the offices that ring the shaft. A simple heating and cooling unit on the roof serves these areas, with supply and return ducts in the skylight shaft wall.

WINDSOR WINERY AT SONOMA VINEYARDS, Healdsburg, California. Owner: *Sonoma Vineyards.* Architects: *Roland/Miller/Associates.* Engineers: *Richard Keith (structural); Williamson & Vollmer (mechanical/electrical).* Contractor: *Todd Construction.*

Ken Howard

FERMENTATION TANKS   CIRCUL.   STOR. BARRELS

SKYLIGHT
OFF.   OFF.
VIEW   TASTING   VIEW

Jeremiah O. Bragstad

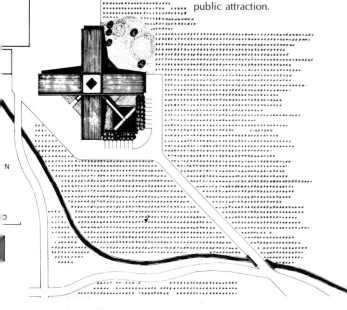

EXISTING STORAGE
BUILDINGS

Balconies adjacent to the
second-level tasting room overlook
the fermentation and wine storage
areas. The amphitheater/picnic area
formed by one of the outdoor
quadrants has become a popular
public attraction.

Jeremiah O. Bragstad

4

Happily for the community of Russellville, Kentucky, the publisher of several local newspapers decided to expand his offices and printing plant in one of the few remaining nineteenth century buildings on the town square. The architects, Ryan, Cooke & Zuern, were asked to study the feasibility of recycling several sites on the square to provide current and future production space. Of some importance was the client's wish that the production of his publications be a visible part of the square's activity. The project was to include 7000 square feet of finished, air-conditioned, expandable space.

The selected location was a combined feed and hardware store that had endured the usual "modernizations." Its advantages —besides a prominent location on the square—included adjacent off-street parking, and a structure that offered positive separation of production and publication functions.

The street facade was stripped of years of various remodelings, revealing the original cast-iron and brick structure. These elements were restored and infilled with woodwork that duplicates the spirit of original doors and trim found stored in the cellar.

The two-story hardware store now houses the publication's editorial, circulation, advertising and management spaces, using an open-office design for immediate convertibility.

The one-story feed store was reworked to accommodate the pressroom and mailroom. Expansion of these two areas will occur in new space erected on the adjoining parking lot.

In the renovation, the existing masonry load-bearing structure could be used. The poplar floors of the feed store were removed and a new concrete slab poured on engineered fill for the presses. The floor boards and structural members were then reused for partition paneling and new stair construction. Plaster was removed from brick walls which were cleaned and left exposed. Existing wood floors and ceilings were simply cleaned, and new mechanical, electrical and sprinkler systems were installed throughout.

Outside, overhead utility lines and lighting were removed from the street facade, and the crumbling walk was replaced with new concrete and brick paving. Street trees were also added.

PRINTING PLANT AND OFFICE FOR THE LOGAN LEADER/THE NEWS DEMOCRAT, Russellville, Kentucky. Owner: *Logan Ink Inc.* Architects: *Ryan, Cooke and Zuern Associates Inc.* Contractor: *Logan Ink Inc.*

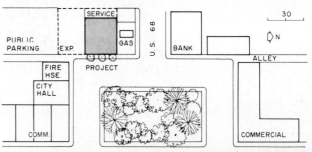

SECOND FLOOR

One half of the second floor
remains unassigned as expansion
for the composition room and a
self-contained news room. When
this expansion occurs, the street
floor will be reassigned for
those business and administrative
tasks directly involving the
public.

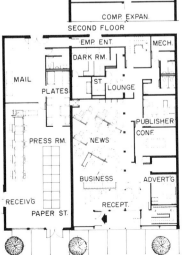

FIRST FLOOR

5

5

Called in to serve two clients—one sensitive to costs, and the other committed to a high standard of design—architects Pasanella & Klein were faced with the task of reconciling in one building the distinctly different goals of a developer and his prime tenant.

The building is the western headquarters of Joseph E. Seagram & Sons in Des Plaines, Illinois. It is a two-story, 75,000-square-foot warehouse with 25,000 square feet of office space containing administration, lounges, lunch room and restrooms.

Departing from the usual arrangement for such buildings—that is, offices to the front, warehouse to the rear—the architects surrounded the warehouse bulk with offices on three sides, giving the three corporate functions within a sense of individuality.

Because the building was needed quickly, the design of the offices was based on readily available, prefabricated aluminum enclosure panels, factory-insulated and finished inside and out. Lightweight steel framing and drywall partitioning completed the offices, which can be applied as modules to the warehouse as additional space is required.

The warehouse—steel framed with brick bearing walls—forms a double-loaded, two-story corridor with the offices (see plan and section). The warehouse roof, slightly higher than the office roof, extends beyond the masonry warehouse wall, covering the coridor and forming a clerestory window. From the outside, the clerestory appears to belong to the warehouse, but really lights the 4- and 8-foot wide corridors, glazed portions of which permit this natural light to be shared by the interior secretarial areas. Although the corridor is used primarily for interoffice circulation, it provides needed office access to the warehouse, which is used for record storage and display building operations.

The saw-tooth, one-story rear portion of the warehouse is designed for special functions and can be expanded with the addition of the second floor.

The centrally air-conditioned building's hvac system located in the warehouse, serves the offices via sheet rock enclosed supply and return ducts that penetrate the warehouse wall, cross the corridor and enter the office space (photo, right).

WESTERN HEADQUARTERS, JOSEPH E. SEAGRAM & SONS, INC., Des Plaines, Illinois. Architects: *Pasanella & Klein*. Structural engineer: *George Kennedy & Associates*. General contractor: *Pletka and Associates*.

Robert Thall photos

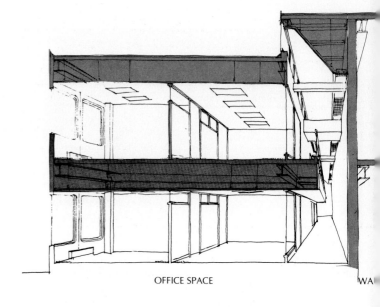

OFFICE SPACE   WA

200

WAREHOUSE

LOBBY

OFFICES

Otto Baitz photos

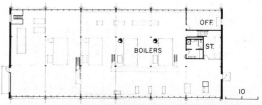

6

Located between two main roads in the community, this 8000-square-foot power plant for a Utica, New York, hospital is intended to be enjoyed by people passing by.

Large glass facades to the northwest and southeast provide good natural illumination and a pleasant view inside. A simple structure of H-section columns topped with large spandrel beams —all in weathering steel—supports the dry gasketed glazed walls. In all, this is a low maintenance, attractive solution to a purely utilitarian building need.

Completed in June 1976, the building is part of a master plan for hospital expansion, and as such can accommodate two additional high-pressure steam boilers. A 13.2 KV electrical system and emergency generators are housed here as well.

The existing plant in the hospital was removed, and a new incinerator put in its place. A tunnel was constructed from the hospital to the new plant.

All work was accomplished without interruption of service to the essential areas of the hospital. After a four-week test period, the new plant was tied into the existing steam distribution network, and the old plant was taken apart.

CENTRAL POWER HOUSE, Utica, New York. Owner: *St. Luke's—Memorial Hospital Center*. Architects: *Rogers, Butler & Bergun—partner-in-charge and project designer: Hussein Shahine; project architect: Joseph Levey*. Engineers: *Snyder, Burns & Associates* (structural); *Richard P. Marche, PE* (mechanical). General contractor: *Charles A. Gaetano Construction Corporation*.

An unusual loft-type building, which produces information as a product, this housing for computors was designed by architects Kahn and Jacobs/Hellmuth, Obata & Kassabaum to fit into a residential neighborhood of Easton, Pennsylvania and still occupy the conspicuous crest of a view-commanding hill on a site of nearly 40 acres. Equitable was willing to go to extraordinary efforts to assure both community acceptance for their 53,000-square-foot facility, and to provide a program and client liaison (through their real estate department) that would assure the desired finished product for an eventual 250 local employees. According to designer Der Scutt, Equitable was one of the most sophisticated clients that the architects had ever encountered.

From the public road to the east (see site plan, overleaf), the building is perceived as an essentially single story solid mass (windows were eliminated in the computer area for security). Parking was placed, out of sight, on the opposite side of the building—and away from the spectacular views from the windows. Despite its apparent solidity, the building is constructed of metal decking on a steel frame, and clad in light brown precast cencrete panels.

Outside of its unusual appearance and the way in which it utilizes its site, the building's principal interest to designers of industrial facilities is the way in which the administrative (small scale) functions have been incorporated into the ''production'' (large scale) portions of the building. As seen in the photos and plan (overleaf), the precast-concrete envelope of the computors' loft has been extended by exposed beams and columns to envelope and contain the multi-level administrative, employee-facility and reception spaces—and thus unify an assortment of otherwise separate parts. This treatment also provides a strong sense of ''opening'' to indicate the entrances.

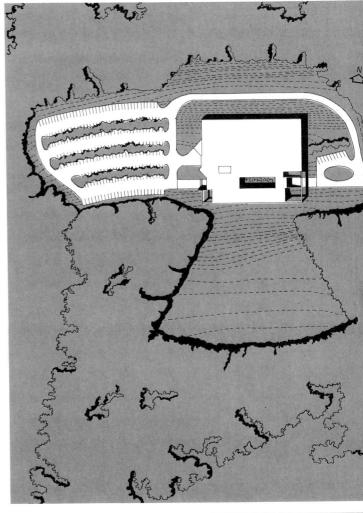

7

Barbara Martin photos

EASTON DATA CENTER, Easton, Pennsylvania. Owner: *Equitable Life Assurance Society.* Architects: *Kahn and Jacobs/Hellmuth, Obata & Kassabaum*—partner-in-charge: *Lloyd Doughty;* project designer: *Der Scutt;* project manager: *Nevio Maggiora.* Engineers: *Weiskopf and Pickworth* (structural); *Woodward-Moorhouse & Associates* (soils and foundations); *Meyer Strong and Jones* (mechanical/electrical); *Clarke and Rapuano, Inc.* (site). General contractor: *Frank Biscoe Company.*

From the approach view (photo, right) the Equitable building is seen as a solid, one-story mass, which extends, by exposed beams and columns, to enclose the smaller scaled offices and facilities (photo above) tucked into the hillside facing spectacular views. The public entrance (at left in photo, opposite) and the matching employee-entrance on the opposite side of the building (top photo at left) are given visual importance as semi-enclosed spaces. Dark glass, in dark frames, neatly spells out "window" (or void) in the solid, light-colored concrete panels of the exterior. The lobby (left) has distant views as well as views into a nearby enclosed court, which acts as an immediate relief to the confinement of the computer spaces, that are brightly colored to create visual interest.

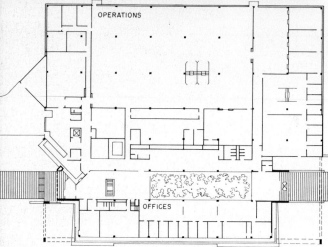

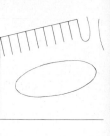

To gain distinction in a surrounding amorphous limbo of industrial buildings and single-family houses, architect Stanley Tigerman has taken a design approach that makes a clear statement of this multiuse structure's existence. For an enlightened speculative developer, Kelmer Arlington Associates, he has consciously created a piece of isolated "sculpture," which—meant to be seen from all sides—stands as an anchor for disparate surrounding parts. Indeed, he was so intent on preserving the monumentality of this example of an often mundane building-type, that he took pains to ensure that no plants would grow against the walls by providing a strip of gravel around the base. The 22,000 square-foot building is meant to look like its original model with flush surfaces and openings.

And the client has every reason to be happy with the results. So universally appealing is the finished product, that it is fully rented, in a competitive market, to tenants who include a fire extinguisher manufacturer and a sculptor. Equally important, its construction cost did not exceed the very low-budget cost allowance established by other industrial buildings in the area. This is largely attributed to minimization of the costs of the basic structure; the concrete block and brick cavity walls of the exterior are load bearing, and one row of pipe columns and beams provides the only intermediate support in the building's 95-foot width. Joists are welded at the points of contra-flexure to increase their practical length of support. An added bonus is increased flexibility due to few interior columns. All finish items —including plumbing fixtures and roof-top air handling units—are supplied by tenants.

The economy of means is a factor shared with many other industrial buildings. But here, there is no real front or back, and a minimal change in appearance from the street (photo, top) to the truck-loading side (bottom). The flat, rounded-box concept is articulated only by the two projecting fire walls.

KELMER ARLINGTON INDUSTRIAL BUILDING, Arlington Heights, Illinois. Owner: *Kelmer Arlington Associates.* Architects: *Stanley Tigerman & Associates—associate-in-charge: Anthony Saifuka.* Engineers: *Raymond Beebe* (structural); *Wallace & Migdal* (mechanical/electrical). General contractor: *Kelmer Arlington Construction Management.*

8

Philip Turner photos

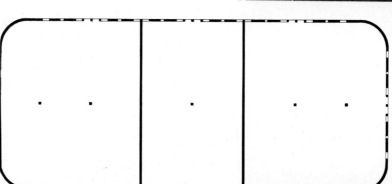

9

The plan, below, and a comparison of the two photos at right shows the extent of the "outriggers" Polshek has added to the existing structure. As they house the Center's four divisions and occur—in varied form—on all sides of the building, they create new elevations which are grafted, with special skill, to the old. A stainless steel batten roof covers the new portions of the building.

The architect notes that the rhythms of the building were easily adapted to the outrigger solution.

George Cserna photos

GROUND FLOOR

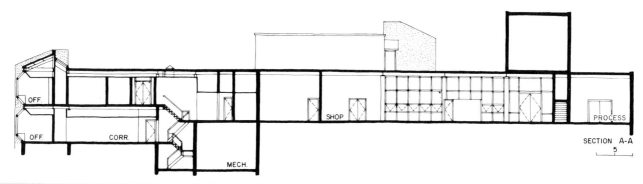

OFF.
OFF. CORR.
MECH.
SHOP
PROCESS

SECTION A-A
5

this addition, the old walls could be punctured, the staff could flow
out to occupy its new outrigger spaces and renovation of the older interior structure could proceed with only minimum disruption to staff
operations or the construction process. Phasing was obviously crucial
and it was worked out by architect and client in the greatest detail
before construction began.

The new outriggers contain office and laboratory space for the
center's four more or less discrete divisions. They have poured concrete
and walls matched to the exterior finish of the existing building. But the
long curtain walls are designed for quick erection and constructed of
aluminum mullions and sections of insulated reflecting glass. (Curi-
ously, this was the first installation of this product in sheets inclined
45 degrees in section). In the two-story portion, photo above, a long
steel spandrel, painted bright red, emphatically marks the division between floors. This outrigger section, as designed, also produces a long
skylight over the coridors that brings daylight into the interior.

In floor area, the outriggers added about 6,300 square feet of new
space. New construction within the existing building comprised another
4,500 square feet and 19,000 square feet of the older structure were
thoroughly renovated.

What Allied Chemical got was, to all appearances, a new building
(containing mostly prime space) except that existing parking, roads,
access, and vertical circulation could be retained to effect important
savings. And because the owners went to Polshek, they got a building
that is rationally organized, sensitively detailed, and innovative both in
the use of materials and in the volumetric treatment of the spaces it
provides.

ALLIED CHEMICAL CORPORATION'S MATERIAL RESEARCH CENTER, Morris-
town, New Jersey. Architects: *James Stewart Polshek & Associates—James Polshek, designer; Dimitri Linard, associate-in-charge; Howard Kaplan, job captain.*
Engineers: *Theodore Kwoh* (structural); *Aaron Zicherman & Associates* (mechanical). Landscape architect: *Johnson & Dee.* Contractor: *The Johansen Company.*

ADMINISTRATION

IBM System Development Division Facility

Manassas, Virginia. Owner: *International Business Machines Corporation.* Architects: *RTKL, Inc. — Ted A. Niederman, principal-in-charge; Joseph L. Scalabrin, project architect.* Landscape architects: *Collins, DuTot & Associates.* Engineers: *Kallen & Lemelson* (mechanical/ electrical); *Van Rensselear P. Saxe* (structural); *Whitman Requardt and Associates* (site).

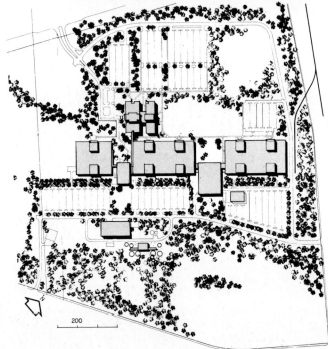

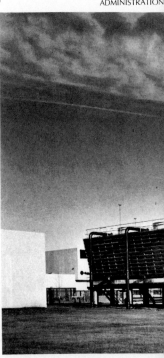

10

Probably no other field demands such a high level of flexibility in all areas as does the rapidly developing field of computer technology. One new development in electronics can create changes in the whole industry literally overnight, and of course, changes, either internal or external, in the buildings that serve that industry. And, of course, the buildings themselves, serving one of the largest and most actively growing segments of industry, frequently start out in the mid-range of project size (a quarter-million square feet) and prepare for further growth.

Therefore, the manufacturing complex

RTKL planned and designed for IBM's System Development Division is architecturally, mechanically, and electrically capable of accommodating a variety of possible changes in manufacturing requirements.

The interior spaces of the buildings have open-floor systems designed on a four-foot module so that internal arrangements can be changed to accommodate future manufacturing, laboratory and administrative needs. A flexible and extensive mechanical system has been provided so that specialized types of environments, including clean room facilities, can be created within the interior spaces. A deep

ceiling plenum contains loops of mechanical, electrical, and plumbing services for changing development and manufacturing needs.

The only permanent spaces within the buildings are main corridors and "core areas" — the locations of stairs, employee lounges, rest rooms and cafeterias. These core areas are strong sculptural elements treated visually to serve as orientation points in the complex.

Color is used in a big, bold way, not only for large graphics but also for textured materials related to the functions performed in the various buildings.

Y   LINK   MANUFACTURING   CAFETERIA

Joseph W. Molitor photos

For those interior spaces that could undergo many changes, a set of standards was prepared for use by the plant management staff. Whenever interior alterations are made in the future, it will serve as a guide as to how color, graphics, furniture, and equipment should be used to be consistent with the design philosophy of the facility.

The entire manufacturing facility is now operational. The engineering facility and smaller administration block shown on the plan will be future expansion additions. A central energy plant and a sophisticated industrial waste treatment plant have been built.

The industrial waste treatment plant has been designed for complete de-nitrification of dilute and concentrated waste which is discharged after processing into the existing stream system on site. The quality of the effluent meets the watershed environmental requirements; the size of the treatment plant makes it quite unique in this country.

The 485-acre site in Prince William County, Virginia is within a half hour of Washington, D.C. via Interstate 66. Anticipating area growth, the planners felt it would be desirable to retain the best of the site's natural features to make it an attractive addition to the area, as

well as to provide the facility with privacy.

It is seldom that a large manufacturing operation can adopt the special concerns for landscaping and effluent control that are ordinarily attributed to research and development facilities. Those matters of social concern, that are of such growing importance in such facilities, are everywhere apparent in this facility, and the vocabulary of assembly buildings reflects the same architectural concern as that of the three-level administration building. Even the cooling towers and high-bay buildings are provided with a setting and detail that respect both social and esthetic objectives.

Robert Brandeis

Kaiser Center
for Technology

Pleasanton, California. Owner: *Kaiser Aluminum and Chemical Corporation.* Architects: *John Carl Warnecke and Associates; Carl Russel, partner-in-charge; Don Schaefer, project manager.* Landscape architect: *Michael Painter (then with Warnecke).* Interiors: *Morganelli, Heumann and Associates.* Engineers: *Chin & Hensolt (structural); Keller & Gannon (mechanical/electrical); Kirker, Chapman & Associates (civil);* acoustical consultant: *Bolt, Beranek & Newman.* General contractor: *Haas & Haynie.*

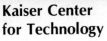

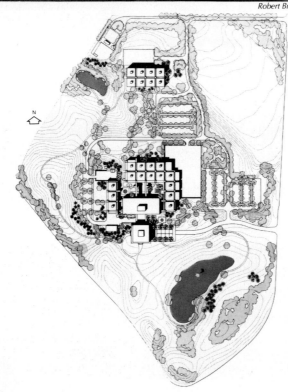

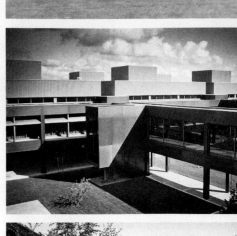

Joshua Freiwald

Joshua Freiwald

11

Landscape as architecture
at Kaiser Research Center

The wedding of building architecture and landscape architecture is seldom more felicitous than it is at the Kaiser Research Center, situated on an 85-acre tract in the rolling hills of the Amador Valley in Pleasanton, California. Alternately called the Kaiser Center for Technology, this complex of six buildings, designed around the expanding demands of interdisciplinary communication, takes notice also of the special character of the research situation. That is, the demands for quiet energy and optional privacy or interplay on the part of re-

search personnel impose a dual architectural problem. First, is the essential grouping and massing of buildings for study, experimentation, and pilot plant operation in such a way as to be separate but mutually supportive. Second, is the imperative of countryside quietude.

The problem, then, for John Carl Warnecke and Associates was not so much the geometry of juxtaposition of the enclaves of discipline for optimum interplay as it was the enplacement of the research universe in compatible union with the world.

The vocabulary of the buildings themselves sustains the Warnecke reputation for

quality and detail. Six major structures enclose a total of more than 300,000 square feet in which a basic 60-foot square module permit uniform division in five-foot increments. The structural system combines reinforced concrete and structural steel. Exterior surfaces are various finishes of aluminum siding or plate and aluminum sun control devices. As with the industrial buildings of all sizes shown on other pages of this report, it is skill in detail and scale rather than the monumental uses of exotic materials that reinforces the architectural presence here.

The administration building with its canti

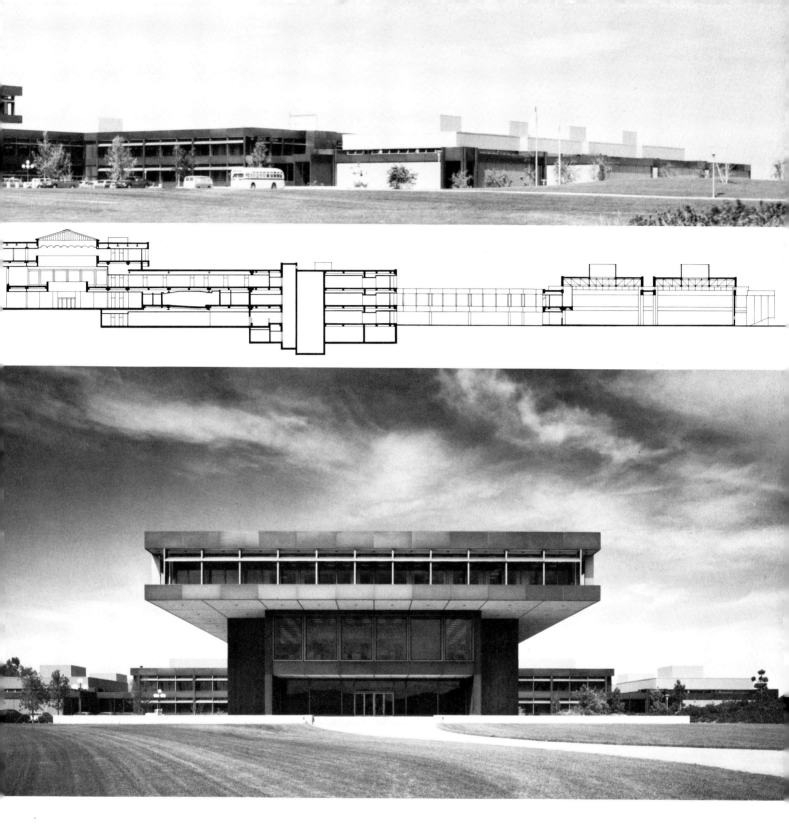

evered top over a main floor reception area surrounds a skylighted well through all floors, reminiscent of some other Warnecke solutions. The three-level main laboratory, the largest structure at the center, houses perimeter offices and a central core of more than 100 bench-scale laboratory modules. Three research divisions and a central analytical department work in this building. It fulfills the purpose of the Kaiser organization in consolidating personnel working in specialties of the corporation in aluminum, chemicals and refractories.

Separate process laboratories were established for each of the three research divisions.

Each has the internal capability of pilot plant operation and introduces truly industrial spaces within the complex. A product development test facility, located quite separately north of the main complex, is equipped to fabricate prototypes of new products and develop specialized tooling for their manufacture.

The role of landscape architecture in this virtually universal mix of industrial and research spaces has been more than the simple embellishment or preservation of existing natural features. Landscape architecture, of course, always participates in the unity of any plan and makes its own contribution to the fulfillment of

program. In this case, however, that contribution carries with it fulfillment of the building architect's own objectives, defined by the client's needs, of an ongoing, expansible campus of facilities respecting its community and purpose.

Architecture touches the lives of everyone around
Success of the total design has received testimony in a letter from the mother of a family who were accustomed to enjoying the countryside on which this technical center was emplaced. The letter is in part as follows:

The Kaiser Center for Technology, like many industrial R&D facilities, engages a full roster of architectural approaches and services. The landscape architect and the building designers unite in a design vocabulary in which the paramount ingredient is talent. The uses of quite ordinary materials in control of ambiance and scale is evident here. The interiors offer the full range from typical high-bay industrial space to the two-level atrium and surrounding offices. Warnecke's interior designer was Jean Coblentz.

Robert Brandeis photos

"To the Planners of the Kaiser building:

"When we first heard you were to put a huge "factory" near Pleasanton, we were sick at heart. We watched sadly as your buildings progressed.

"When the grounds were landscaped my young son said, "Look, mother, it's not ugly! It's pretty!" When the fountain was completed, he reminded me each time we passed how wrong I had been until it became a thing with us to say "Bucky's Water" each time we went to town—from the oldest to the 18-month-old. A week before Christmas we lost our Bucky, he was ten years old.

"Life goes on and we still go to town. The youngest, now close to three, chants "Bucky's Water" and so it will always be. Bucky is in Pleasanton Memorial Garden on the hill overlooking your buildings and lovely grounds. For I was wrong. The countryside is truly more beautiful than it was." Marjorie L. Santos.

D. J. McPherson, vice president and director of technology at the center, replied, with grateful compassion, saying in part: "Since moving into our new research center our employees and residents of surrounding communities have enjoyed our lake and fountain. In the rush of getting settled, however, we never

have given the lake a name. With your permission, Mrs. Santos, we would be honored to name it "Bucky's Water.""

McCue Boone Tomsick's Santa Teresa Laboratory, in California, is a new feather in the cap of IBM's increasingly long list of significant architecture. Specifically for computer programmers, the complex contrasts nature and an appropriately efficient and shiny machine image — but while it is taut and disciplined, the complex presents a kaleidoscope of vistas, colors, reflections and patterns.

12

This big, handsome complex for the General Products Division of IBM (used by 2000 persons, mostly computer programmers) solves a long list of seemingly incompatible problems. These, in abbreviated form, include providing for (and doing the most for): a beautiful, but earthquake prone, natural setting; a large group of technical people needing both extreme efficiency and compensating human comforts and pleasures; and the highly special and demanding requirements of computers. The result is unusually good architecture—very distinct from, but also very friendly with its surrounding world.

Extensive analysis of the programmer's work patterns indicated that nearly 30 per cent of their time was spent working alone, 50 per cent with groups of two or three persons, and the balance with larger groups or carrying out other responsibilities; and a typical department consists of ten to fifteen persons.

Armed with this and masses of other data, the architectural design team led by Gerald McCue worked through a series of design schemes and cost analyses. From among these studies, a campus-like set of eight cruciform-shaped buildings surrounding a plaza met most of the users' requirements—in particular, the client's request for private offices for the programmers, with as many as possible oriented to the outside views.

The design of an effective circulation pattern became extremely important once this "campus" configuration was selected. All buildings are linked beneath a second level plaza, which is a prime contributor to the "non-institutional" atmosphere of the complex. Most of the buildings are also linked by bridges at the upper floor levels. The core of each building contains the stairwell, elevator (in five of the buildings), restrooms, and "administrative support centers," surrounded by the primary circulation corridor. Radiating from the core are

Jon Naar

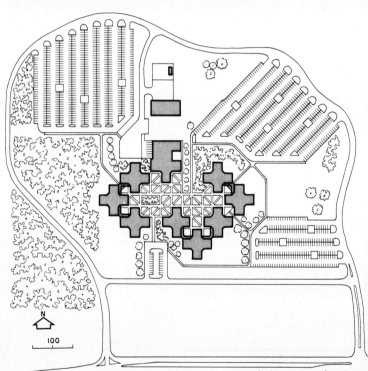

Named after surrounding Santa Teresa foothills, the complex is built on 50 acres of 1,180-acre site contained within a loop road serving as a possible fire break. The facility consists of eight four-story office towers—all having a cruciform shape—and a low, two-story building containing kitchen/cafeteria and power house, totalling nearly 600,000 square feet. All buildings surround an open, formal plaza, which is level with the second floor of the office towers. Below the plaza is the computer room, lobby, library and small, open court linking the first floors of all the towers.

identical arms of private offices, a large conference and common computer terminal room, all serviced by a secondary U-shaped corridor. Therefore, all corridors are short, no longer than 50 feet, with no office more than 15 feet from a window.

The clustering pattern of three buildings offset from the other five marks the entrance from the visitors' parking area and reduces the scale of the complex from the roadway. It also creates a variety of spaces on the plaza, including six courtyards between the buildings, and directs views from the plaza outward to the hills on the north and to the valley on the south. Furthermore, this organization opens up "vista corridors" diagonally and at right angles throughout (seen from within the office towers as well as from the plaza), and views are architecturally emphasized by grass-lined or paved walkways on the plaza level. From certain locations, one can see the buildings' forms march down the slope of the site or across the plaza quadrangle (left), or perceive a surrealistic view of the landscape framed by buildings across the plaza.

The complex was designed to withstand expected earthquake forces. A moment-resisting steel-frame structure, it is dynamic, capable of moving relatively freely in an earthquake. The buildings' skin, therefore, needed to be lightweight, and the aluminum was chosen for that and its high reflective quality. Mirror glass—set flush with the aluminum curtain wall panels—complete the total reflectiveness of the facade, while contributing to the over-all energy-conscious design.

The structure harmonizes with the site through its scale and proportions. "The building was meant to flirt with the landscape," says McCue. "It does not try to change it. The building ought to become an interesting contrast . . . [for] it is the juxtaposition of the man-made forms and colors to nature's . . . [that] heightens the intrinsic values of both."

Shown are six interior courtyards (above) that are formed when two cruciform-shaped buildings come together in the designed cluster pattern. The courtyards act as colorful gateways to the buildings from the plaza level.

The facade has the incredible ability to reflect—often abstractly—movement on the plaza as well as weather patterns, from the gray of early morning fog to brilliant light on a sunny day, to the golden colors of late afternoon. A subtle aspect of the design, but one with tremendous visual impact, is that the outside corner of each building is beveled at a 45 degree angle, which emphasizes each corner by reflecting light in a thin line.

Each building is color-coded with brilliant colors (magenta, red, red-orange, orange, yellow, green, teal and blue) for building identification. The coding is complete, from office tack boards to stairwells, carried to the exterior only where the wings of two adjacent buildings form a courtyard. Therefore, there are two colors in each courtyard, predetermined as complementary pairs.

This is an energy conservative design, including the use of solar reflective glass. Heat generated from the buildings' lighting systems and from the primary computer room—a one-acre area below the grand expanse of plaza—is recovered and used to heat water, which is in turn pumped to all eight buildings (all computer controlled for optimal efficiency). In addition, every room in the complex has its own light switch for individually controlled light use.

Marvin Wax Photos

A typical perimeter office (top) is oriented to outside views. The cafeteria (left), located in the only two-story building in the complex, is large and open, capable of serving and seating all workers, for few people leave the complex for lunch because of its location at the edge of town. Outdoor eating areas are furnished with colorful red tables and sun-shades (not shown). The fourth floor plan is identical to the third level, being distinguished from the second level plaza area in that only the upper stories have bridges connecting most towers for easy circulation.

IBM SANTA TERESA LABORATORY, San Jose, California. Architects: *McCue Boone Tomsick (now MBT Associates) — principals-in-charge: David C. Boone and Alan R. Williams; design team: Gerald M. McCue in-charge; Philip Copland, Kyle Cumbus, John Damonte, Gerald Dommer, Linda Groat, Charles Jennings, Ron Jewett, Tully Shelly.* Engineers: *Forell/Elsesser Engineers (structural); John V. Lowney & Associates (soils); Gayner Engineers (mechanical/electrical); George S. Nolte and Associates (civil).* Landscape architects: *The SWA Group.* Interior design/graphics/costs: *McCue Boone Tomsick.* Consultants: *Bert Marshall Jr. (food service); Eugene O. Tofflemire and Associates (curtainwall).* Construction managers: *Swinerton & Walberg.*

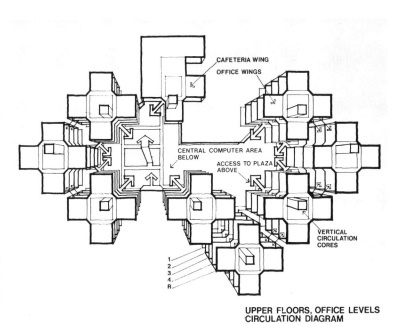

CAFETERIA WING
OFFICE WINGS
CENTRAL COMPUTER AREA BELOW
ACCESS TO PLAZA ABOVE
VERTICAL CIRCULATION CORES
1
2
3
4
R

**UPPER FLOORS, OFFICE LEVELS
CIRCULATION DIAGRAM**

Index

√U

760855